DAVID
MAASS

TEXT BY MICHAEL McINTOSH

THE WILDFOWL ART OF DAVID

MAASS

BRIAR PATCH PRESS
CAMDEN, SOUTH CAROLINA

This book and other volumes in
Masters of the Wild are produced by
Briar Patch Press, Inc.
P.O. Box 770, Highway 521 S.
Camden, South Carolina 29020.

BRIAR PATCH PRESS, INC.

John Culler: *Publisher*
Charles A. Wechsler: *Editor*
Kay Kennedy Jackson: *Design Director*
Hugh C. Howie, Liz L. Strohl, and
Genia L. Weinberg: *Graphic Designers*

Printed in Italy.

ISBN 0-922724-15-6

(Previous Page)
Coming In – Blue-winged Teal, Oil, 24 x 32, 1989
(Dust Cover, Front and Back)
Greenhead Alert, Oil, 24 x 36, 1987
Golden Bounty – Canada Geese, Oil, 24 x 36, 1989

To Ann,
who comes unequaled as a wife
and as a mother. Because of her
love, understanding and
unselfish devotion, I feel I am
better – both as a painter and as
a person.

To Jenni and Paul,
because children are what life is
all about and I've been fortunate
enough to have two of the best.

ACKNOWLEDGMENTS
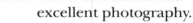

Publishing a book of this magnitude, complete with reproductions of paintings that span over two decades, would not have been possible without the generous contributions of several talented individuals and their companies. Special recognition to: Walter (Buzz) Peck and Brown & Bigelow, Inc., for sharing color transparencies of Dave Maass' calendar art; and to Bill Meyer and Sara Koller of Wild Wings, Inc. of Lake City, Minnesota, for providing transparencies of paintings published in limited edition. Also, thanks to Jostens, Inc. of Owatonna, Minnesota, for allowing us to reproduce the artist's design for the 1963 U.S. Air Force Academy class ring. And finally, to Steve Peck of St. Paul for his excellent photography.

Migrants – Pintails, Oil, 24 x 32, 1987

When I first started painting back in the early fifties, I had no idea where my newfound hobby would take me. While I knew there were a few artists who were actually making a living portraying wildlife, it never occurred to me that I would someday join their ranks. It hasn't been easy. I have often been told that artistic ability is a great gift — a God-given talent. For me, it also involves a continuous struggle. There are days when all my efforts seem futile, and I continue working into the night trying to solve what appears to be a simple problem. However, in spite of long hours, hard work, and occasional failures, many people have heard me say that I would not trade my life with anyone!

When asked to write a dedication *and* a foreword, I was immediately struck with the difficulty of separating the two. There are so many people, friends, and relatives alike, who have played such an important role, not only in assembling this book, but in helping me with my career. It would be impossible to list each of you individually, but this book would seem somehow incomplete without a special word of thanks and appreciation to all of you.

I am particularly grateful for the support of my family. As a young child on hands and knees with pencil and scratchpad, I was never discouraged or told that I was wasting my time. Instead, there was more likely to be a "Hey, that looks pretty good!" The encouragement that began back in those early years continues today.

It was a tremendous honor to have been asked by Briar Patch Press to participate in this *Masters of the Wild* series of books. To be placed alongside such a distinguished group of artists is to me both very humbling and a tribute which ranks second to none.

A special thanks goes to Mike McIntosh who made working together a pleasure. His outstanding literary ability enabled him to organize and convey my thoughts as well as could possibly be done.

DAVID MAASS

INTRODUCTION

Dave and I have been good and close friends for many years. Although we've talked about a world of things, we've never really spent much time on art, especially his — because I have great respect for his unnecessary modesty. So now, when he isn't face to face, I'd like to speak for his numberless friends and thank him for what he's done. To bless him for the evenings and the afternoons and the dawns he's shared with us; to express our delight at his gift of his creatures that we can carry home — their heads cocked just so, their passing untroubled by our presence and their radiant loveliness forever preserved.

Dave has been enshrined in more dens, studies, duck camps, and living rooms than any other artist that I know; with good reason. Having his art displayed makes a statement about ourselves as sportsmen. He says for us that we *understand* the beauty, the rituals, the mystery and the affection that are part of the emotional complexity of gunning.

A sky full of Maass mallards or canvasbacks needs to be looked at carefully for a few minutes. The eye discovers that no two birds are in quite the same attitude, no two birds have quite the same striking of light or shadow. Dave's genius is giving us the subject in varying degrees of exposure, a near cinema effect so as the eyes flow across the painting, we feel life. In the set of a head or the angle of flight, he tells us there is urgency. Or with the wings back as comfortably against the wind as we might adjust ourselves to a favorite chair at home, he tells us there is calm. I have the feeling, looking at David's work, that before he was here to show us what we need to see, there was nothing, and that when we turn away the place will be empty again. His work provides a magic minute — a vision, that had he not seen it and held it for us, would never have been so perfect.

David leaves us with an idea of beauty that goes far beyond the physical image. I see in his art all that I love about being there. I find the reasons that make the hours I spend listening and watching and feeling, being a part of the wild, return to me whenever I need or want them.

Among my many favorites is *Misty Morning Woodcock*. Here Dave takes a

place and converts it into a dream, an ideal, a place better than real and puts in it the essence of what the woodcock is; a flash of beauty, a wild thing held forever; not only does the eye rejoice but the heart gladdens at the revelation, seeing it for the first time, as often as we wish. This is what art is all about — holding a moment against the force of time, keeping a vision, a glance, a glimpse of the unseeable, where we can always find it.

Every so often a man appears and shows us that this is what we are really seeing. This is the essence of intellect — or art. This is what David Maass has done for us — to show us a common thing in an uncommon way, to let us hold it in the eye as you would a diamond in the hand, turning it so it catches the light, first one way and then another until the magic of it becomes obvious — and then we can never see it again as plain and ordinary because it isn't anymore; it has become wondrous.

GENE HILL

Misty Morning – Woodcock,
Oil, 24 x 28, 1968

13

CONTENTS

Hazy Ascent – Mallards, Oil, 26 x 38, 1988

THE TRAIL FROM THERE TO HERE

At five o'clock every morning, David Maass laces on a pair of running shoes and covers three miles at a brisk trot. A blizzard might keep him indoors, but little else will, not rain nor sultry summer heat nor the piercing cold of a Minnesota winter. David Maass begins his day with a run through the weather.

A couple of hours later, he's at the drawing table or the easel, the weather beyond the windows all but forgotten, for somewhere in David Maass' mind, the world is always on the cusp of winter.

It's a world of wind and water, of flighting ducks, pheasants in the snow, and grouse on misty mornings; a world of rich autumn color and gray winter chill; a world as old as migration, as new as hope. It's a world out there, in the weather.

It's a lovely, subtle quilt of a world. At the edges, you'll find a patch of Arkansas, a snippet of the West, bits of North Carolina and the Atlantic coast, and some swatches of Canadian marshland. The center, though, belongs to Minnesota. Except for a brief but significant period in the early 1950s, David Maass has always lived in Minnesota — in Rochester, in Owatonna, on Fish Lake near Waterville, and now on Lake Minnetonka, west of the Twin Cities. But the connection goes deeper than residence alone, deeper than landscape, deeper than weather, for that world in David Maass' mind is the world of a hunter.

You can see in the man something of the boy that David Maass once was. He's there in manner — watchful, quiet, a bit shy perhaps — but nowhere does that boy come more vibrantly alive than in David Maass' smile, a smile so genuinely warm and open that only the sourest spirit could resist smiling back. Other than the lines in his face, graven by a lifetime out in the weather, his fifty-nine years could be fifteen or twenty fewer, for all they show. He has sixteen years on me, but seeing us both reflected in the glass of his Ramcharger as we met at the airport in Minneapolis, it occurred to me that a guess on appearances alone might well reverse our ages.

When I mentioned that sometime later, Dave's wife Ann jokinly suggested that writers live more dissolute lives than artists do. She might be right; in any case, being well into a second martini at the time, I was in no position to argue.

Any writer who wouldn't enjoy driving through Minnesota with Dave Maass on a fine morning at the end of May probably is beyond redemption, but I'm not that man. From the airport, we headed southeast along the Mississippi, bound for Lake City and lunch with Bill Webster, president of Wild Wings and Dave's longtime publisher and longer-time friend. With each mile unrolling

Dave Maass in his log cabin-studio on the shores of Lake Minnetonka near Minneapolis-St. Paul.

smoothly behind us, we also headed back into time, for southeastern Minnesota is where the story begins.

avid Maass was born in Rochester on November 27, 1929, just over a month after the first shock waves of the Great Depression jarred the American Dream and two days before Commander Richard Byrd became the first man to fly a plane over the South Pole. By about 1933, when even the northern prairie country began to feel the weight of hard times, Arthur and Ora Maass' son had found an interest of his own in airplanes, and horses as well, drawn on scraps of paper and presented, as young boys will do, to his mother. Ora Maass was fond of horses. David Maass, as it turned out, would be fascinated lifelong by things that fly.

"Birds have intrigued me for as long as I can remember," Dave said. "Every kid loves wildlife, almost any kind. I certainly did. But something about birds really took my fancy."

Something, indeed, about birds — wild, free little spirits, familiar as leaves and yet ultimately mysterious, exotic in their power of flight. Who has not at one time or another imagined himself a bird and envied such freedom from the struggle and crush of an earthbound life? Who at times has not longed simply for wings?

In the mid-1930s, there was much to fly from. Mired in the pit of economic depression, the nation struggled to hold itself together while optimism and hope drained slowly away. Even the hardiest

spirits bent under the stress, and many of them broke.

"I don't have any particularly bad memories of growing up during the Depression," Dave said. "But it was the only world I knew, and as any kid would, I suppose I simply accepted the fact that the world was a tough place to get along in. My parents knew what it was like to live in better times, and I'm sure it was harder on them than it was on me.

"Even when my parents divorced — I was about seven at the time — it wasn't as if the world had come to an end. I wasn't happy about it, of course, but neither of them stopped caring about me, and they made sure I knew that."

Both Arthur and Ora Maass remarried, and with both families living in Rochester, Dave maintained a close relationship with his father and his stepmother, Elizabeth.

Ora Maass' second marriage proved to be a turning point. Kelly Jacobs owned a dental laboratory in Rochester and an enormous love for the outdoors.

"Actually, Kelly and my mother both loved shooting and hunting. Kelly managed the Rochester Gun Club, and we all spent a lot of time there, especially on the trap range. My mother, in fact, was Minnesota state trapshooting champion in 1948.

"I never really got excited about target-shooting — probably because I never did much of it. When I worked at the gun club, my job was loading the

From top: Art Maass and his new-born son in the early 1930s; Dave as a toddler; and mother, Ora, at the time she won the Women's Division of the Minnesota State Trapshooting Championships.

19

trap. I suppose if I'd spent as much time shooting as I did in the trap house, I might have liked it better.

"What Kelly really loved to do, though, was hunt and fish, and he took me along whenever he could. I wasn't old enough for hunting yet, so at first we fished together."

Dave's smile flashes. "For a while, Kelly didn't own a motor for the boat — but he didn't need one, since he had me. I must've rowed a zillion miles with him. I'd troll a bass plug along behind, and he'd stand in the bow with his flyrod. He bought a little Evinrude later on; I've been fond of outboard motors ever since.

"Kelly was everything I could ask for in a stepfather. He was a great Dad. I probably would've discovered hunting without him, but it might not have meant so much. I'm glad he was there to show me what it's all about.

"I was twelve when he took me duck hunting for the first time. It was on Weaver Marsh in the Mississippi River bottomlands. It was really cold, the marsh almost frozen.

"We rowed out to a little bay that Kelly thought would be a good place and worked the boat back into the rushes. He had about a dozen wooden mallard decoys, old Herter's blocks, and by the time he set them out and got back in the boat, I could hardly sit still. What with being there before

Dave's stepfather Kelly Jacobs and Ora in the early '80s. It was Kelly who introduced Dave Maass to hunting and fishing.

daylight and going through all the preparation and everything, it seemed as if something tremendous was about to happen."

As it turned out, something was.

"The first ducks came in just as it was light enough to see, light enough to shoot. Kelly took the first ones. Actually, I was so struck by the sight of those birds barreling in out of nowhere that I didn't even lift my gun.

"The ducks kept coming, teal and wigeon and bluebills, and I finally started shooting after a while, although I wasn't doing much more than making noise. Kelly was a splendid shot. Every time another flock came in, he'd kill one or two while I was blazing away, and then he'd grin at me and say, 'Good shootin', Davey!' I believed I killed one duck. That was a wonderful day."

For some, hunting never lets go. We measure out our lives along contours shaped by hunting days and by the people with whom we share them. Like art, hunting connects us with dimensions of reality inaccessible in other ways and acts as a doorway to contact with the natural world. Also like art, hunting celebrates moments that, held in memory, provide solace against the mutability of time.

"Kelly and my mother and I spent opening day of the duck season one year on Rice Lake, not far from Owatonna. I can still remember the wind and the way it churned up whitecaps on the lake. I especially remember my mother shooting two teal, two blue-wings; they came tearing past, the way teal do, and she turned, calm as you please, and shot them both.

"You know, I can't tell you how many days I've spent hunting ducks — hundreds, at least — but I remember that day and those two teal as if it happened this morning."

While David Maass, under Kelly Jacobs' tutelage, was learning to be a hunter, others recognized in him the spark of artistic talent. In the Depression years, as in the war years that followed, few small-town Midwestern families owned the wherewithal for private instruction, but as sometimes happens, the right help came at the right time. From a grade school teacher, herself an amateur artist, he learned how line and shadow could lend depth to a two-dimensional plane. From high school art teacher Charles Rudkin came more sophisticated challenges and technique. From David Maass himself came a growing wish that art could somehow be more than a pastime.

"I had an idea that I wanted to be an artist, but I didn't have a clue how anybody went about making a living at

it," Dave said, shifting his chair to shade his eyes. We were on the deck at his house, taking the noonday sun like a couple of well-fed bears, watching Lake Minnetonka glitter through the trees across the lawn, and talking about how we came finally to do what we do.

"I'm not even sure I knew what a freelance artist was, much less how to be one. There I was, a high school kid in Rochester, Minnesota, which was a nice place to be, but it didn't seem like the best place in the world to sell paintings. I didn't know who'd buy 'em anyway. Did you have any idea how to be a writer?"

"Not the foggiest. I was a high school kid in Ottumwa, Iowa. I thought if you wanted to be a writer you had to go to New York and starve to death in some rathole apartment. All the publishers were in New York, and I guess I thought you had to deliver manuscripts in person."

"Did you go starve in New York?"

"I managed to miss that pleasure, somehow. Besides, I wised up and learned that the real way to be a writer was to be a teacher and write the Great American Novel in my spare time."

Dave raised a questioning eyebrow.

"Well, I did teach for a few years, anyway."

Dave laughed. "How'd we ever get from there to here?"

*D*ave came by way of class rings and the U.S. Marine Corps.

Like many another high school student with a talent for drawing, he found himself part of a committee responsible for designing a class ring and securing a manufacturer. It was a simple enough job, since Josten's, Inc. of nearby Owatonna has long been a major supplier of such items, but it opened a door to David Maass' future.

"When I visited Josten's on that class-ring project, I discovered a way to make a living as an artist — by working in the design department.

"I applied at Josten's right after graduation. Robert Hahn, who was the design director, felt I didn't have enough experience and encouraged me to enroll in an art school and then try again for a job.

"So, I applied at the Minneapolis School of Art, and they turned me down, too. That

Maass (second from left) in his photography class at Rochester High School, 1947.

21

was 1947, when schools were giving preference to World War II veterans. The art school was full.

"I wasn't sure what to do next, so I enrolled in a correspondence course through the Minneapolis Art Instruction School. I finished three lessons."

Short-lived though it was, his career as a correspondence student was not without a measure of success, for years later, the school granted David Maass an honorary degree.

"I had my mind made up to work at Josten's, so I went back. This time, I applied for any job they had, figuring that if I got my foot in the door, I'd be there when the next opening in the design department came along."

A few weeks later, David Maass was working full-time at Josten's, operating a pantograph in the tool and die department. After six months, he was

promoted to pattern cutter, and a year and a half after that, nineteen years old and newly married, he found the niche he was looking for in the design department.

"It was good training, all of it. The pantograph and the pattern work gave me a good mechanical background, and the design department was where I really learned to draw. Designing jewelry is precise work. It taught me to think in three dimensions, and it taught me to be accurate.

"Every good painting, regardless of the style or the technique, begins with good drawing, because that's what gives it form and structure. The more I worked at designing rings and school insignias and such, the more accurately I could draw, and that's been the basis of the work I've done ever since."

Enter, once again, the right person at the right time. Just as David Maass was hitting his early stride as a designer, Stu Ferreira hired on at Josten's. An ex-Marine with a brand-new master of fine arts degree from Northwestern University, Ferreira was a hunter, a fisherman, and a wildlife artist. He also had an eye for talent.

"Dave was the best designer in the place," Ferreira says. "All the illustrators used the same media, but you could recognize one of Dave's drawings instantly. Nobody could handle light the way he could, even then."

Common interests led to friendship. "Stu and I spent a lot of time together, hunting and just knocking around

outdoors. He was doing wildlife paintings in his spare time, and I learned a great deal just watching him work."

Having the formal, university training that David Maass lacked, Ferreira could offer technical advice, but the friendship proved more important. "Dave had far more talent than he knew. All he really needed was some confidence in his own ability."

"Stu kept encouraging me to paint. I really didn't think I could do it very well, but he kept showing me new techniques, nudging me into trying them. He's been a great friend."

When the painting began in earnest, it came from a longing in the heart, from a yearning for home.

In 1952, warfare echoed from far-flung corners of the world. The French Union Army thrust northward in an obscure southeast-Asian country called Vietnam; British troops landed in Kenya to face the bloody Mau Mau uprising; and American soldiers struggled and died in the freezing landscape of Korea. Certain that he'd be drafted, David Maass enlisted in the U.S. Marine Corps.

"I fully expected to be shipped overseas right after boot camp. I ended up assigned to the Marine Corps photography lab in San Diego and spent my whole two-year hitch right there."

He also met his first art collector in

San Diego, a senior drill instructor with a taste for cheesecake pinups. "He had some pinup girls tacked on the walls in his billet. I remarked to somebody that they weren't very well-drawn — which they weren't. He overheard me and asked if I thought I could do better. I said yes. Jeez, I thought I was going to get reamed, but he looked at me for a minute and then told me that my job was to make one new drawing every night until he decided he had enough.

"I guess he liked them, since they were still on his wall when I left boot camp."

The training and experience in photography later would prove valuable, but hours in a darkroom pass slowly for one who prefers to be out in the weather. And San Diego, though pleasant enough, isn't the fine countryside of Minnesota.

"I really missed Minnesota. My wife was with me, so I wasn't lonely, but I wanted to be home, to go duck hunting with Kelly or shoot some pheasants with Stu, or just paddle around the lake and fish."

A chance meeting in Balboa Park revealed yet one more turn in the trail.

"We went out to the park one Sunday afternoon and discovered an open-air art show. One display in particular caught my eye — wildlife paintings, ducks, geese, grouse, woodcock — birds I hadn't seen since I left Minnesota. My tour of the show stopped right there. We looked at every piece and then got acquainted with the artist.

'I'd never heard of David Hagerbaumer till that day, but I thought he was a superb artist. We spent the rest of the afternoon and most of the night talking with him. We've been friends ever since."

Out of the tedium of military life, laced with a longing for home, came David Maass' first serious wildlife art — drawings, pastels, and then, with Hagerbaumer's encouragement, watercolors and paintings in casein. Big cats sketched at the San Diego zoo soon evolved into game birds drawn from memory and set against backgrounds that always looked like Minnesota.

"The more I monkeyed around with casein paint, the more I wanted to try oil. I didn't know how to handle oil, so I wrote

Opposite: Maass in the photo lab at Marine Corps Base in San Diego. Stu Ferreira became a close friend and essential adviser early in Maass' art career.

Above: 1953 oil painting of canvasbacks; the artist in his first "studio," one corner of his bedroom in a San Diego apartment.

A 1954 oil painting of shoveler ducks.

to Stu for advice. He wrote back and advised me to come see him whenever I could get back to Minnesota."

On a thirty-day leave shortly after, Ferreira offered David Maass his easel and a challenge — copy in oil a pair of canvasbacks from the back of a playing-card.

"I still have that painting, and every time I look at it, I can remember how frustrating it was to try handling oils, especially when Stu made it look so easy. I'd smear paint around for a while, then ask Stu how to get what I was after; he'd take the brush and solve the problem with about three strokes.

"Actually, there are a few really good things in that piece. They're all Stu's.

"I took some tubes of oil back to San Diego, though, and fought with the damn things every spare minute I had, painting nothing but game birds. By the time I left the Marine Corps, I was beginning to get some control over the paint.

"It was a wonderful hobby. It still hadn't occurred to me that I could ever make any money at it."

Owatonna, 1954: "It felt good to be home. I went back to work at Josten's as a senior designer and decided that my goal was to become head of the art department. I kept painting, evenings and weekends, because I enjoyed it. Stu was always there to help me solve technical problems. I'd talked with him and Dave Hagerbaumer about selling paintings, but then I did get promoted to art director at Josten's, and that kept me busy enough that I didn't pursue the other.

"Kelly actually sold the first ones. He'd put two paintings — one of wood ducks and the other canvasbacks — on display in a store window in Rochester. A couple from Washington, D.C., saw them and called him. He quoted a price at a hundred dollars apiece, and they bought both of them.

"I sold another one the following year, and then, in 1956, Kelly suggested trying a bigger market, like Von Lengerke & Antoine in Chicago.

"That was scary. It was a big, high-class sporting-goods store, and I had no idea whether my paintings were good enough to get even a second glance there. I talked with Dorothy Terp, who was in charge of the VL&A art department, and asked her to look at my work and give me some advice.

"I took seven paintings to Chicago, figuring that I'd bring them right back home again. But Dorothy liked them and agreed to take the whole bunch on consignment. What surprised me even more, all seven sold, and Dorothy asked if I'd send some others."

Word soon got around that the new kid from Minnesota was worth a serious look. As the second consignment of paintings began to sell in Chicago, both Ralph Terrill, managing director of Crossroads of Sport in New York and Ed Thomas, art-buyer at Abercrombie &

Fitch, put yet other David Maass paintings on display. At the time, Crossroads of Sport and Abercrombie and Fitch were perhaps the most important sporting-art galleries in the country. The prodigious Maass talent had not yet set the art world afire, but it was burning brightly enough.

Busy days, the late 1950s — a full-time job at Josten's, freelance painting, and in November 1957, a daughter.

"Jenni was a delight — she still is, as a matter of fact. Kids have so much energy; I'd get charged up just from being with her.

"I needed it. By the early '60s, I was turning out as many as seventy paintings a year. They were all selling, which of course made me want to do even more, but having what amounted to two full-

time jobs was too much. It was taking away time that I wanted to spend with my family or out hunting or just keeping my own energy level up.

"I'd thought about leaving Josten's, but you know what it's like to cut loose from a dependable income and start freelancing full-time. That fear keeps coming back: 'What if this doesn't last? What's going to happen a year from now?' I had a family to look after, and I wouldn't have risked their security for anything.

"They were supportive, though, and so were the people at Josten's, who gave me a half-time schedule so I could spend more time painting. When that still didn't solve the problem, they went even further and kept me on the payroll as a consultant. I was really flattered by that. I've always been grateful for the opportunities Josten's gave me and for

Maass in 1955 with Robert D. Hahn, director of design at Josten's, the country's largest producer of custom-made rings. Maass' designs for 1963 class ring at the U.S. Air Force Academy.

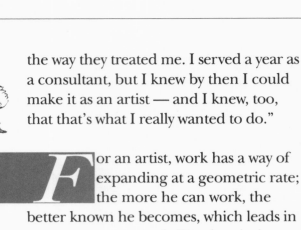

the way they treated me. I served a year as a consultant, but I knew by then I could make it as an artist — and I knew, too, that that's what I really wanted to do."

For an artist, work has a way of expanding at a geometric rate; the more he can work, the better known he becomes, which leads in turn to yet more work. Dave's paintings were selling in satisfying numbers through the galleries in Chicago and New York, and commissions began to come along as well.

"A lot of clients wanted paintings of their favorite hunting spots, and I did quite a bit of traveling on commissioned pieces, doing location research. I met some wonderful people that way. But there also was a problem, as I discovered.

"Crossroads of Sport had published a catalogue of original paintings including some of mine. If someone called to inquire about one that was already sold, Ralph Terrill would suggest that he commission me to do another. Quite a few people did, but a lot of them wanted pieces just like the ones they'd seen in the catalogue.

"Naturally, I could change some details — put the birds in different positions, change the clouds, things like that — but I found myself painting essentially the same scene several times over. It takes a lot of effort to recast the same material and make it different enough each time that you don't lose the enthusiasm and the spirit.

"It got to be an even bigger problem later, when some of my older paintings were published as prints. Having very similar prints available is confusing to viewers and also leaves the impression that I only do one painting over and over. That happened to some degree early on, and since then I've had to be careful not to let too many look-alikes get into the print market."

Dave hitched a deck chair closer to the table. Sunset drew long shadows across the lawn. "What do you like best about being a writer?"

"Getting paid for enjoying sundowners with people like you."

Dave laughed.

"Actually, I'm serious," I said. "Or mostly serious. I like the work for its own sake — the same reason you like to paint — but the best part is being able to earn a living doing the things I'd do in my spare time if I had some other job."

"Yeah," Dave said. "You're absolutely right. Just being able to hunt ducks is great, because I love to be out there, but being able to relive the experience by doing a painting, and making a living at it ... that's really great."

"The company isn't bad as a fringe benefit, either," I said.

"We do meet really interesting people," Ann said. "It's been especially good for Paul." Paul, fourteen and starry-eyed for boats, was on the dock at the moment, cranking his new Boston whaler onto the lift after a turn around Maxwell Bay. "He's been able to meet a lot of people that most boys his age don't — artists, even some writers; he's met Gene Hill and you."

"Two perfect specimens of the

breed," I said. "Fine examples for any mother's son."

Ann wrinkled her nose. "Which is why mothers get gray hair at an early age."

"It's funny how experience and work feed each other when you're lucky enough to combine the two," Dave said. "The paintings that mean the most to me are the ones I can associate with certain places and the people I was with. A couple of the Arkansas pieces, for instance, are special to me because that's where Ann first came duck hunting with me, and there are quite a few paintings that remind me of hunting with Arnold."

David Maass and Arnold Krueger met in Owatonna thirty-five years ago, two young men with a common love for the exquisite misery of duck hunting.

"Arnold knew some pretty good places to shoot, little out-of-the-way spots that often drew ducks when not many other places did. As a matter of fact, the first time we ever hunted together was in a spot like that.

"It was late in the season. Everything was freezing up, and I'd just about quit hunting for the year. I ran into Arnold in town one day; he said he was still getting some good shooting and invited me to join him. Next morning, we went out on one of the lakes where he'd found some open water off a little weedy point.

Dave Maass with Arnold Krueger, a good friend, hunting companion, and neighbor in southern Minnesota.
From left: Dave and wife Ann with Sherry and Larry Grisham on a duck hunt in Arkansas. Maass had just served as a judge in the World Calling Championships at Stuttgart.

Maass and his Irish setter Toby in 1975, hiking the winter woods above his former home at Fish Lake.

"We had all our decoys and gear in Arnold's canoe, and we pushed it out across the ice like a sled. The ice wasn't very thick yet, which concerned me, since I was only wearing hip boots. Arnold said not to worry, that the water was only about a foot deep where we were.

"Maybe it was only a foot deep where he was, but it was about three feet where I broke through the ice. A bootful of cold water sure wakes you up in a hurry.

"Other than that, it was a terrific shoot. I had some dry socks in the truck, which was a good thing because it was about fifteen degrees that morning. Both our guns kept freezing up. We had a kerosene heater in the canoe that kept our hands and our guns reasonably warm, but when the shooting is really good, you don't pay much attention to the cold. It was that good, bluebills just piling into the open water.

"Arnold and I have hunted together ever since. When I moved to Fish Lake several years later, Arnold bought a farm just a few miles away and started developing it as a wildlife project, improving the habitat, building all kinds of structures to expand the wetland and control water levels and such. We both tried to get quail established on our places; he had better luck than I did, but the winters here can be rough on quail.

"His wetland project turned out beautifully, though, and I've done quite a few paintings with Arnold's place as the setting. We don't see each other as often as we used to, but we always hunt ducks together on opening day, something we've done for years."

Funny, indeed, how experience and work feed one another. Experience means more paintings to do; more paintings mean wider recognition and new opportunities for yet more experience, new turns in the trail. By the mid-1970s, Jimmy Robinson had joined the growing number of people who found special appeal in David Maass' work.

He was all but a legend by then, Jimmy Robinson was: *Sports Afield* journalist of forty years' standing; champion of North American waterfowl; tireless promoter of the shooting sports; friend of presidents, movie stars, and celebrities of every stripe, from Annie Oakley to Babe Ruth, Clark Gable to Ernest Hemingway. He was a ceaseless talker; trader of tales; public-relations man extraordinaire; altogether one of the great characters of the American sporting world.

"Jimmy lived in Minneapolis, and I'd run into him several times at DU dinners or art shows or affairs of that kind. Of course, everybody knew who Jimmy Robinson was. He was always complimentary about my work, both to me and to other people.

"Among all the other things he did, Jimmy managed the *Sports Afield* Duck Camp on the Delta Marsh in Manitoba, and in the mid-'70s, he invited me to come up and hunt with him. That was quite an honor, because he was very selective about who he invited.

"Unfortunately, I couldn't go that year, nor the next. There was always some work I felt I needed to get done. Jimmy knew me well enough to know that I

Never at a loss for words, genial Jimmy Robinson shares a story at his duck camp on the Delta Marsh in southern Manitoba. Maass and Jimmy again, with Byron Webster (left), director of the American Museum of Wildlife Art, and Len Samuelson, a senior vice-president for Ducks Unlimited. The occasion was a banquet in honor of Samuelson, a Minneapolis resident who has been active in D.U. for years.

Top: Friend Don Dahl with Delta Marsh guide, Leonard Lavalle.
Above: From left, guide Frank Lavalle, Ron Schara, outdoor editor for the Minneapolis Tribune, *Maass, and Tony Soderman of Orono, Minnesota.*

wasn't playing hard to get, and he finally took the classic Jimmy Robinson approach — called me one day and yelled, 'Dammit, Maass, stop being a mole in a hole! Quit hibernating, and come shoot some ducks with me.'

"So we went, I and my old friend Don Dahl, who was a Minnesota State Patrol pilot. We flew up to Portage La Prairie and then went on to Delta by car. There were maybe a dozen other hunters, but Jimmy took us in like we were his long-lost nephews.

"We hunted in pairs, two hunters and one guide per boat, and the first morning Jimmy decided that I was going to shoot with him. I'm not the world's best shot, and I felt a little intimidated at first — my God, I'd grown up reading Jimmy Robinson's stories, and here I was duck hunting with him. But of course, I went, Jimmy and I and Frank Lavalle, who was Jimmy's number-one guide.

"We rowed out to one of his favorite spots, a place the guides called Jimmy's Point. I had a great time. Jimmy had a knack for putting people at ease — he hardly ever stopped talking, for one thing — and I shot well enough that I didn't embarrass myself. Not as well as Jimmy did, though; he was almost eighty years old then, but it didn't take long to figure out why he was a member of both the skeet and trapshooting halls of fame.

"It was a wonderful experience, shooting at Delta. I went back several times, and I've done a lot of paintings from those trips. In fact, that's where I took Paul for his first duck hunting a couple of years ago. Hunting with Jimmy was always a treat. There's never been anybody quite like him."

True enough. No one ever accused Jimmy Robinson of lacking a sense of himself nor of failing to play the character-role he created, but there was genuine substance to the man. And there can be no question that he held a great affection for David Maass. It's unmistakable in his letters, hacked out on an obviously well-used manual typewriter with a breezy disregard for the nuances of spelling, punctuation, structure, coherence, tidiness, and form — letters that might end in the middle and restart in a stream-of-consciousness that James Joyce would have envied. For instance:

Dear Dave,

Did you send John Wayne a wood duck? xxxis Can't recall. Hope you get some ducks. If not, give me a ring and I'll take you to Elbow Lake next week — if you want to come, ring me. Best to the better half,

Your friend,
Jimmy.

Come down some night for dinner. Any time. While at the duck camp — Bob Huffines, one of the owners of ABC — who hunts with me every year said he met you last year with Eugene duPont —

did you remember him? Used to have a big plantation in SC — sold it and now lives in Pinehurst, NC.

Had a letter from Alex Kerr, who owns the Kerr Sports Shop in Beverly Hills — a great guy and great friend — (also owns Kerr jars) He said, "I would like to sell some of Mass Paintings — his address is Alex Kerr — Kerr

Sport Shop — 9584 Wilshire Blvd. Beverly Hills, Calif. — sells a lot of paintings — one of the nicest stores I have seen — his photo is in all of my books.

He sild your Wooduck as soon as he got 'em. You shoud have had 4,000, insread of 2,000 — everybody wants 'em. I could have sold hundreds at the Grand.

As always,
Jimmy

And again:

Sir David Maass

Arrived week agao last Saturday glad to get the Hell out of town- Tell Don that Clara was again arretsted for speeding at Thief River Falls. U sould have seen the lok on her face. I was delighted as I had told her a fewmiles back to cut down- but you know these dam women.

Never saw so much water xxxxxaround here for years. Ducks in every pot hole and we have some great hunting here, but I dont knowabout out west or sothern Man. where i here it is very dry in some places.

Clara isin Sask. c visiting relatives- called the other night and aked me how I was feeding. "A dam sight better than you feed me," I said. Had corn flakes for breakfast- a hot dog for dinner. "Told her to stay as long as she like because Frank and I were dxxxng doing OK px nobody to say "Clean up that mess, Jimmy, "Jimmy do this, Jimmy do that. Frank the same. She had a new roof put on before she left- I stayed inside and watched.

Wht dont you run up for a few days- tou and the gal some weekend and watch the mud hens hatch out.

Best and take care
Jimmy

Maass and Jimmy Robinson after a successful shoot on Jimmy's Point.

A few days after Jimmy Robinson died in 1986, a billboard appeared in Minneapolis, the space donated by some of those who had called him friend. The message, edged in black, read "Jimmy Robinson/ 1897-1986/... The Memory Lives On."

Along with it was an enormous reproduction of a painting that shows a flock of bluebills winging in on a flat prairie marsh. Anyone who'd seen the piece before would have no trouble recognizing *Jimmy's Point* by David Maass.

Maass' painting, Jimmy's Point *(page 110-111), on commemorative billboard purchased by friends of Jimmy Robinson.*

The setting here is the marsh adjacent to the home of my friend Arnold Krueger. I painted it just a few years after he put in his dams and other water-control structures; you can see that the trees are dying as the marshland expands. Flooded timber that's beginning to die out is ideal wood duck habitat.

I showed the ducks flying off to take advantage of the drakes' colors. The water is glassy to echo some of the intense blue from the birds in the reflection of the sky.

Mirrored Solitude — Wood Ducks,
Oil, 26 x 38, 1986 (© Brown & Bigelow, 1988)

This is Fish Lake in southern Minnesota, where I used to live, and in fact, it's the lakeshore right in front of my house. It was bitter cold the day I took the background photos for this painting. I shot the pictures in the morning; in the afternoon, it got down to about five degrees and the lake started to steam. The wind died down that night and next day it was frozen over. I think the wind was the only reason there was open water.

The day I chose to show in the painting is cold but not terribly windy; this is late November, good bluebill weather.

As any duck hunter knows, bluebills usually break in toward you, come almost head-on, and then flare off at the last second. These birds are flaring; there's no sense here that any of them are going to settle in.

The most interesting challenge in this piece was the foreground, getting the snow drifted up in rolls along the cattails and keeping everything clean and sharp. And the ice just beyond, which is either forming or breaking up, depending on the wind.

The New Arrivals — Bluebills,
Oil, 24 x 32, 1985 (© Brown & Bigelow, 1987)

Doves seem to be plentiful just about everywhere, but I wanted to paint this little flock in a Southern setting — Georgia, the Carolinas perhaps, somewhere in the South. I also wanted to use fairly strong colors, not necessarily bright ones but strong, since the mourning dove's coloration is quite subtle. The spotted tailfeathers are about the only significant markings they have, so I painted the two foreground birds with their tails fanned, as if they're about to break into the aerial maneuvering that doves are so good at.

Winged Flurry — Mourning Doves,
Oil, 24 x 32, 1986 (© Brown & Bigelow, 1988)

This painting actually started with the maple tree and all the brilliantly colored vines growing on it. I considered several different birds, some as bright as the tree, but none seemed quite right. That tree is so striking that a brightly-colored or even strongly-marked bird would take something from it — and vice versa. I finally decided to go the other way and chose a bird with understated plumage.

Alert Pair — Mourning Doves,
Oil, 24 x 32, 1982

(© Brown & Bigelow, 1984)

ometimes simpler is better. I always have enjoyed painting skies, the challenge of getting a certain drama in a cloudy sky without relying too heavily on color.

I prefer to approach sky as a design problem. In the drawing stage, I kept rearranging the birds and tinkering with different cloud patterns at the same time, looking for just the right composition, trying to make the various shapes come together in some harmonious way.

Winging Over — Canada Geese,
Oil, 26 x 38, 1984 (© Brown & Bigelow, 1986)

As in few other states, Arkansas' duck stamps are done on commission rather than chosen in open competition. Both the species of duck and, to some extent, the location are specified as part of the commission. This particular setting represents the Black River area in the northern part of the state, and shows the sort of dead-timber habitat that attracts a lot of ducks in Arkansas.

For the birds themselves, I was trying to capture a sense of the fast, zig-zag flight common to teal. They are almost unducklike in their size and flight, but they're certainly interesting to watch.

The Arkansas duck stamp program has been in place for nearly ten years now—1990 is the tenth anniversary—and it's been extremely beneficial for waterfowl, particularly since Arkansas has so many ducks and is so popular among duck hunters. Sales of both stamps and prints, which are published by Larry Grisham of Jonesboro, have raised a lot of money for waterfowl conservation. I've been invited to design the tenth anniversary stamp, and I'm looking forward to it.

Arkansas Duck Stamp — Green-winged Teal,
Oil, 13 x 18, 1983

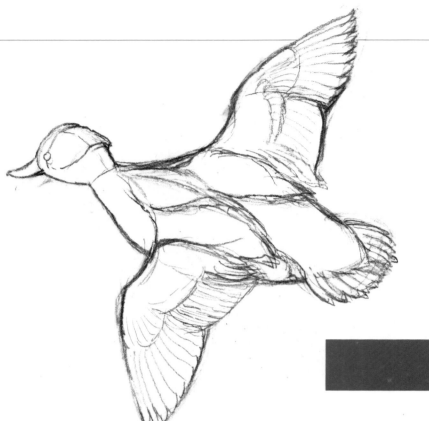

This is transitional weather — that brief time when a storm is just breaking, or something similar. I was interested in showing the lake in the transition between late fall and winter, between open water and freeze-up. The shallow water along the shoreline is frozen, but there's still open water farther out.

I thought buffleheads would be appropriate for this time of year, since that's when they often show up here. The drakes are particularly interesting because they are so strongly marked. Their pitch-black and brilliant-white colors, when viewed from a distance, almost seem to pulsate as the birds fly across the water.

Up and Away — Buffleheads,
Oil, 24 x 32, 1983 (© Brown & Bigelow, 1985)

*A*long with pheasants and gray partridge, chukars represent one of the most successful attempts at importing foreign game birds to North America. Chukars seem to resist cold weather better than our native quail, and like pheasants, they are well adapted to otherwise bird-poor habitat across the northern Great Plains and into the mountain foothills of the West.

Although dressed in the exotic plumage of their native Asia, chukars are essentially quail-like in shape and behavior. They live in coveys but generally fly as a group when they flush, rather than scattering in all directions as bobwhites do. Their strength on the wing makes them excellent game birds, both in the wild and on shooting preserves.

Maass' treatment captures not only the bird's handsome appearance, but also its gregarious nature and the rugged foothill terrain typical of chukar habitat.

First Snow — Chukar Partridge,
Oil, 24 x 32, 1988 (© Brown & Bigelow, 1990)

47

Ring-necked ducks are named for the faint brownish neckband which appears only on drakes. Waterfowlers often refer to the birds as "ringbills," because both sexes have a prominent white ring near the tip of the bill.

Ringnecks look and behave somewhat like bluebills, but they seem to prefer the shallow wetlands where you typically find puddle ducks. These birds are descending into the wind, flaps down, packed together in typical diving duck formation.

Passing Through — Ring-Necked Ducks,
Oil, 24 x 32, 1977 (© Brown & Bigelow, 1979)

By the early '70s I had come close to winning the federal duck stamp competition several times, certainly close enough to keep up my enthusiasm for entering each year.

I liked the spirit and sense of movement in the birds, and had a feeling that the piece would finish well in the competition. Even so, it was a wonderful surprise when they called to tell me I'd won. There's no thrill quite like winning the federal.

1974 Federal Migratory
Bird Hunting Stamp — Wood Ducks,
Oil, 6 x 9, 1973

ven though I seldom paint a human being into a scene, I usually try to imply some human presence, try to bring the viewer in as part of what's happening in the painting. Something has startled these quail — a hunter perhaps, or someone else.

I think of quail as farmland birds, and I usually try to establish that connection in quail paintings, hence the old abandoned house and barn. I suppose you could think of the human presence here as two-fold, both in space and time — the viewer in front, the old farmstead in the background; the viewer now, the farm in the past.

Startled Covey — Bobwhite Quail,
Oil, 24 x 32, 1981 (© Brown & Bigelow, 1983)

eeing a black duck is a special treat here in the Midwest. They show up occasionally, one or two flying with a flock of mallards, but we don't see the numbers you'd find on the East Coast.

Black ducks are wary birds, which is something I wanted to suggest in this painting. At least three of these ducks are settling in — and the two that are farthest away may do the same — but a couple of others look as if they're going to flare. It's hard to fool an entire flock of black ducks.

This is a typical East Coast marsh, good habitat for lots of species. Certainly, it is the sort of place where you'd expect to see a flock of blacks coming in.

In to Feed — Black Ducks,
Oil, 24 x 32, 1980 (© Brown & Bigelow, 1982)

*B*lack brant are West Coast birds, from Alaska on down. They're among the smallest of geese, not much larger than mallards, and they seem to like flying low to the water, either in broken-vee formations or in long strings.

I didn't have any certain spot in mind here, other than to make it look like some Western coastal marsh. I was mainly interested in the design aspect, in getting a pleasing pattern among the birds, and in unifying everything by arranging the reedbeds so the shapes and patterns of the birds and the background echo and amplify each other.

Ragged Formation — Black Brant,
Oil, 24 x 32, 1980 (© Brown & Bigelow, 1982)

This is a Lake Minnetonka scene, a bay we found when we were out puttering around in the boat one day. I liked the old shack in the background and the composition, with the broad patch of lilypads leading back to tall rushes.

It's early fall, and I have to confess that I cheated just a little on the ducks. At this time of year, drake ruddy ducks would have little of their rust color. But I wanted to keep that, to show them in mating plumage, and I also wanted to get some of the early fall colors in the trees and the rushes. So I took just a bit of artistic license.

The water was a challenge — to contrast the ripple in the foreground with the calmer surface among the lilypads. Back there, the plants break up the breeze, so the water is smoother and reflects more than the foreground water does.

I placed the horizon line high, because I wanted plenty of room in the foreground to develop the water and the birds and the various layers in the composition from front to back.

(Detail) *Viewed from several feet away, a Maass painting appears somewhat detailed. But closeup, we see a surprisingly loose, almost carefree style. A series of quick slashes becomes a stand of cattails. A swirl of green becomes a lily pad. A dab of umber becomes the reflection of distant trees. Then, too, is his use of lively, clean colors which in concert, give an impression of reality.*

Tranquil Setting — Ruddy Ducks,
Oil, 24 x 32, 1988 (© Brown & Bigelow, 1990)

*E*ven though I don't generally use bright colors, I seldom do a painting as monochromatic as this one. Gadwalls are often called gray ducks, so I decided to do a whole painting mainly in shades of gray — gray birds, gray weather, gray water, no color in the setting any more intense than the brightest color in the birds themselves. I was challenged to see how much vibrancy and spirit I could get with a limited, fairly drab palette.

Marshy Maneuvers — Gadwalls,
Oil, 24 x 32, 1986 (© Brown & Bigelow, 1988)

*D*oerr Pool, in Whitewater Wildlife Management Area in southeastern Minnesota, provides ideal habitat for waterfowl. I used to spend quite a bit of research time in the Whitewater, and I always liked the Doerr Pool area for the visual effect of dead and dying timber.

I made this a rather gloomy morning, with enough haze to soften out the distance but not so dense that it would obscure the river bluffs. Those hills along the Mississippi and its tributaries are landmarks in that part of the state; it's hard to think of the Whitewater without thinking of its majestic limestone bluffs.

Moving Out — Gadwalls,
Oil, 24 x 32, 1981 (© Brown & Bigelow, 1983)

I did this on commission for Tom and Dawn Wanous, who have a summer home on Lake Superior, just south of Grand Marais. This little point of rocks is right in front of their house.

Lake Superior, the world's largest body of fresh water, draws concentrations of migrating waterfowl, mostly bigwater ducks like goldeneyes, buffleheads, and even harlequins.

The contrasting textures and shapes of the water and rocks were interesting to paint. The rocks allowed me to imply the water's depth and power, even though the waves themselves aren't very high.

In many of my paintings, the birds play a more dominant role, simply because I am trying to convey something about their behavior, or character, if you will. But here I chose to make the birds less conspicuous, so the viewer can get a stronger feeling for this immense lake and its rugged coastline.

North Shore — Goldeneyes,
Oil, 24 x 36, 1980

*I*n the northern grasslands, sharptails are the most widespread of the prairie grouse. Unlike prairie chickens and sage grouse, they seem to prefer some diversity in their habitat, for they are most often found in brushy coulees or near small stands of trees that have managed to establish outposts in a world of grass and sky.

Like all ground-dwelling birds, the sharptail's coloration matches the environment where it evolved–which, as Maass shows here, comprises muted grays, browns and faintly buff-colored white. Its name derives from the pointed central tailfeathers, and its broad wings, designed for fast takeoff and gliding flight, make the sharptail a splendid game bird.

This particular spot isn't far from Portage la Prairie in Manitoba. The day I found it, I was out with Jack Barrie, a former Royal Canadian Mounted Police officer and a wonderful wildlife photographer. We were exploring the countryside and shooting photos, and this struck me as a good scene for a painting.

Sudden Takeoff — Sharptail Grouse,
Oil, 24 x 32, 1984 (© Brown & Bigelow, 1986)

Bill Webster and I came up with the idea of a series of paintings that showed both the ducks and the habitat typical of each one. We decided to start with this scene of mallards in the Central Flyway.

Obviously, there's considerable variation in flyway habitats from north to south, but each of them has certain identifiable features. For the mallards, I chose a tributary along the Missouri River, which to me typifies the Central Flyway.

There's a certain basic theme that carries through all four pieces, something to unify them as a series, but not so strong that each painting can't stand on its own. Basically there are three principal, foreground birds in each, with others in the background to imply that a lot of waterfowl use these areas.

Although this is the Missouri Basin, I wanted to make it a place where someone might say, "I think I've been there." I wanted to leave a little mystery in it, to let the viewer bring his own experience to the painting.

Mallards — Central Flyway,
Oil, 28 x 24, 1986

*T*his is a cornfield in southern Minnesota that I kept planted for pheasants and deer. It's the same field where I show the two birds in the *Early Winter Morning* pheasant painting; if you stood by the fencepost in that one, you'd see this view of the field and my neighbor's farm in the distance.

The cornfield always looked pretty beaten-up toward the end of winter, knocked around by weather and animals. It never was the kind of clean field that you see in most areas of the Midwest, but the wildlife certainly liked it. I'd often see pheasants there and always liked the way they looked on bright mornings against the snow.

A Touch of Winter — Pheasants,
Oil, 24 x 36, 1986

I love to paint ducks on rough-weather days, with squally skies and choppy water. Canvasbacks and redheads are among my favorite subjects for bad-weather paintings, mainly because they're two species that don't mind moving around in high wind. Being there can be cold and miserable, but a sight like this, redheads slamming across the marsh, heading into the wind, is worth just about any amount of discomfort.

I spent a lot of time arranging the birds so they would appear realistic, yet visually pleasing. There is no distinct horizon line in this painting, only a few scattered clumps of bulrushes. So to provide a feeling of distance, I separated the birds into small flocks extending from foreground to background.

Into the Wind — Redheads,
Oil, 24 x 32, 1981 (© Brown & Bigelow, 1983)

66

*H*ere we have typical grouse country: a deep ravine with grouse sort of playing follow the leader down into it.

I was trying for depth and distance without using a particularly long view to achieve it. Hazy backgrounds tend to foreshorten perspective somewhat, but I wanted to see if I could use the haze and still get the distance.

Approaching it as a matter of design, I decided that a feeling of looking downhill would achieve the effect I was looking for. And I believe, in this case, that the mist enhances the illusion of distance.

This is one painting that ended up almost exactly the way I planned it in the beginning. That doesn't always happen, but it always feels good when it does.

(Detail) The trickiest part in painting birch trees is getting them dark enough. In direct sunlight, birchbark is brilliant white. But the shadow side doesn't really look white to the eye, so you have to paint it fairly dark. This also helps to convey the illusion of roundness, which can be another problem altogether. Sidelighting tends to make curved surfaces appear flat. To make a tree look round, you have to manipulate direct light against reflected light, with the deepest shadows in between.

Canyon Crossing — Ruffed Grouse,
Oil 36 x 30, 1988

*A*t the south end of Lake Manitoba, a short drive from Winnipeg, the Delta Marsh is some of the finest waterfowl habitat in North America–fifty-six square miles of cane, bulrush, cattail, and water. It lies in the heart of the prairie pothole region, the great duck factory where ten percent of the continent's breeding area produces at least half of the continent's ducks. Delta Marsh is the crown jewel of it all.

The millions of waterfowl that use the marsh as breeding ground and migratory staging area have for years drawn hunters and biologists, writers and artists. Few have captured the essence of Delta, both as a landscape and a biome, so well as David Maass. Though the marsh formed only recently in geologic history–some ten thousand years ago as the last glaciers retreated–there is a timeless quality about the view we get of it through his eyes.

In those views, Delta Marsh is water and wind and grass under a vast bowl of sky, a world of weather and wildfowl, where variety and change are subtle but continuous.

Windy Flight — Pintails,
Oil, 24 x 32, 1984 (© Brown & Bigelow, 1986)

Prior to painting this design, I spent some time off the coast of Maine, both to get a feel for the environment and to learn something about common eiders. I referred to some videotape of flying birds so I could study their attitudes in flight. I worked from study skins to refine color and detail.

Eiders aren't like other ducks; they look different, fly differently, and their group behavior is different. They have bulky bodies, stubby tails, wings set farther back than most ducks', and trail their feet out behind as they fly. They also carry their heads lower than other ducks do, almost lower than their bodies. In flocks, they fly close to the water, seldom fly over land at all, and move around in strung-out groups. Fascinating birds.

In the final design, I used the Pemaquid Lighthouse to define the location specifically as Maine. All in all, I think it's one of the strongest stamp designs I've done.

1985 Maine Duck Stamp —
Common Eiders,
Oil, 13 x 18, 1984

I always associate swans with big country, maybe because they're the largest of our waterfowl. I don't often use mountain settings, but it seemed appropriate for these birds.

The perspective, too, is unusual among my paintings. I chose it to get what I thought would be an interesting view of both the swans and their environment. I don't believe this angle, with the viewer higher than the flying birds, would work very well anywhere but in the mountains. I prefer paintings that don't keep the viewer up in the air, so to speak. To me, a representational painting should offer a perspective that is likewise realistic. In this case, looking down on the subject works, because the viewer could actually be on top of a nearby peak and have the swans flying below him.

Regal Flight — Tundra Swans,
Oil, 24 x 32, 1982 (© Brown & Bigelow, 1984)

In this painting, I was equally interested in the environment as well as the geese. Ricefields are wet, muddy places, and I wanted to capture as great a sense of that as I could. It's tricky sometimes to make a piece of masonite look like water and thick, squishy mud; I find I can do that best using oil paint and working it wet on wet.

To enhance the feeling of depth, I made the fog fairly dense and graded the values among the birds, keeping those in the background little more than shapes in the distance and grading through to the foreground geese, which are painted in full value with just a bit of sunlight on them.

Low Ceiling — White-fronted Geese,
Oil, 24 x 36, 1987

This is a companion piece to the whitefronts and to a third painting I did on the same theme, which featured Canada geese. The flooded cornfield could be Minnesota or North Dakota or Iowa or just about anywhere you'd find snow geese—or snow and blue geese, as they're often called. Snows and blues actually are just different color phases of the same species.

They like to feed in big flocks, so I painted quite a mass of them in the background. Those on the ground are painted rather simply, but with enough detail to make it clear they're feeding.

In keeping with the *Low Ceiling* theme, I imparted a wet, flat landscape and let the heavy weather create different planes of intensity from the background forward.

Low Ceiling — Snow Geese,
Oil, 24 x 36, 1985

ere I set out to feature the birds more than the background. I wanted a clear sense of heavy weather and wind and strong wave action — all to emphasize how powerful canvasbacks are. There's some rough weather here, but there's scarcely any weather that'll keep canvasbacks from going wherever they want to go. They're that tough. It's the kind of day canvasbacks like — or at least the kind of day I like to imagine they like. Not many birds are more impressive than a bull canvasback.

Homeward Journey — Canvasbacks,
Oil, 24 x 32, 1988

There are lots of mountain ash trees in northern Minnesota, and I usually associate them with winter grouse. Mountain ash berries stay on quite late, sometimes nearly through winter.

The bright red berries against fresh snow struck me as a colorful and interesting element, so I decided not to include any more background than necessary to convey a sense of the birds' environment. I wanted the grouse to be perched rather than flying — wanted them more connected with their environment than with some implied human presence.

Early Winter Morning — Ruffed Grouse,
Oil, 36 x 30 1982

(Following Page)

This was Maine's first duck stamp and the first of three that I did on commission for the state's Department of Inland Fisheries and Wildlife. The department chose the species for all three stamps, and I agreed that black ducks were good subjects for the first one. They're magnificent birds, typical of the Atlantic Coast, but their numbers have declined over the past years. Several states, Maine among them, have taken special measures to help bring back the populations. I was happy for the chance to help promote that effort.

1984 Maine Duck Stamp — Black Ducks,
Oil, 13 x 18, 1983

POWER OF
THE PRESS

*T*wenty-five years ago, the market for wildlife and sporting art was a tiny backwater of the art world. For the most part, those who wanted a piece bought an original, either from a gallery or by commission directly from the artist. Few galleries specialized in wildlife art, and it was not unusual for an entire year, or even two, to pass without a wildlife art show being held anywhere in the country.

Wildlife art prints scarcely existed at all. A handful of pieces issued by even fewer publishers supplied the entire market, such as it was. No one took prints very seriously, anyway; they were, after all, "pictures" of art, certainly not "art" itself. Prints were decorative perhaps but of little enduring value, ultimately dispensable.

Now, of course, the situation is vastly different. Wildlife art is immensely popular, and prints are the cornerstone of the market. Once you could almost count all of the print publishers in the world on one hand; now, a pocket calculator can scarcely keep up with those in the United States alone. Many are skillful, some are inept, and a few are truly superb in both the taste and the quality of their products. Taken together, they are key players in what now has become a multimillion-dollar industry.

Prints make art accessible, and that certainly has been the case with wildlife art. Those who cannot afford several thousand dollars for an original often can spare a hundred-odd for a print, and if the printing itself is properly done on high-quality paper, the buyer gets good value for his money. As the concept of publishing limited editions has contributed even further to validating the print as a serious form of art reproduction, a thriving secondary market has grown up around what not so long ago was a largely insignificant enterprise.

David Maass is a pioneer of the genre and one of the most widely published wildlife artists of all time. For him, it began with calendars.

"In the early '60s, the Lewis Howe Company, which manufactures Tums, asked me to supply some paintings for calendar reproduction. They wanted hunting scenes, a hunter in the background and a game bird of some sort in the foreground — images they could reproduce as calendar cards and distribute to drugstores as giveaways.

"Then about 1964, Shedd-Brown, a calendar company in Minneapolis, commissioned me to paint birds. They'd have the printer run off twenty-five or thirty extra copies of whatever painting I'd done for them and give them to me. I'd sign those and give them to friends as gifts.

"Every once in a while, somebody would offer to buy one, someone who wanted something I'd done and couldn't afford an original, and that gave me the idea that prints might have some real possibilities."

Crossroads of Sport published two David Maass prints in 1966 — a canvasback and a grouse.

"As I recall, Crossroads ran about four hundred copies of each piece, and they sold pretty well. Three years later, Frost & Reed, which is a British print house, ran another series; Crossroads marketed those, too.

"Even so, I didn't get wholly serious about prints until I started working with Bill Webster."

More clearly than most in those early days, Bill Webster saw vast potential in publishing wildlife art. A southeastern-Minnesota duck hunter like David Maass, Webster in the 1950s was among the small coterie of collectors who specialized in duck stamps and the then-few prints that accompanied them. As more Maass paintings came into public view, the more intrigued Webster became by the talent they demonstrated.

"Bill traced down my address and simply knocked on the door one evening. He introduced himself, said he understood I was an artist, and asked if he could see some paintings. That was 1960. We took a liking to one another right from the start.

"He bought a painting, a woodcock piece, and we kept in touch. Not long after that, he commissioned a waterfowl piece. Bill lived at Frontenac, on the Mississippi, and he wanted a painting of

This pair of green-winged teal became the official logo of Wild Wings, Inc. The Minnesota publishing house released its first Maass print in 1973, and since then, has reproduced over 100 other Maass paintings.

canvasbacks at Willow Point, which is right below his house and one of his favorite duck-hunting spots. I liked the place, too, from the first time I saw it, looking out toward the bluffs on the Wisconsin side of the river, and that's how I painted it. Always a great place to find canvasbacks."

In the early '60s, while David Maass was in transition from jewelry designer to full-time artist, Bill Webster began to envision a career change of his own.

"I was a salesman at that time," Bill says, "working for the Master Lock Company. Wildlife art was a hobby, one I dearly loved. My marketing sense told me there was potential in art publishing, but I wasn't sure how to get it rolling. The field was so new in those days; there wasn't much to go on."

The notion finally hatched in October 1967, brought to life by four men hunting woodcock.

Bill Webster: "John Dill, an old friend of mine, owned a cabin in Pine County, and we invited Dave Maass and Dave Hagerbaumer to join us for a couple of days' hunting. Neither of them had ever hunted woodcock, by the way…"

Dave Maass: "The first bird we found got up in front of me, and I shot it. I was used to shooting ducks, and this weird little bird seemed so easy to bag that I started wondering what all the fuss was about. I couldn't see much sport in it.

"Then I missed about twelve birds in a row and changed my mind. I've loved woodcock ever since."

Warmed by the fire and good whiskey, what do four hunters, half of them wildlife artists, talk about?

"I told them about my idea for publishing art," Bill Webster says. "We kicked it around for two days, and by the time I got home, I was more convinced than ever that it could work. I asked my father, who was also interested in the idea, what name we might give to a publishing house, if we had one. We made our own list of possibilities, and there was one that occurred to us both.

"That's how Wild Wings came to get its name. But it was born in that cabin in Pine County."

It grew in a tiny room above Bill Webster's garage, nurtured by Webster and his father and Gloria Fitchen. Now, Wild Wings is a chain of galleries and one of the most important wildlife art publishing companies in the world.

"We started slowly," Bill says, "and didn't actually turn out the first print until 1970 — a quail piece by Owen Gromme. We wanted to be sure we were doing it right. It took time to find the right artists and the right printer, set up a marketing system — lots of things to do."

Wild Wings published its first David Maass print, *Back Bay Mallards,* in 1973. All 450 copies readily sold. *Misty Morning — Woodcock* (pages 12-13) followed shortly after, a piece that would bridge the past and the future.

"I was thinking about that first woodcock hunt with Bill and John and Dave Hagerbaumer. The birds intrigued me, and I had such fond memories of the trip, so I decided to do a painting just as I remembered it, with the woodcock and the birches and the misty atmosphere in the morning woods. The experience meant a lot to me, and I was pleased with the way the piece turned out."

"We published it as an edition of 450 prints," Bill says, "and every one of them was gone in a matter of weeks, sold out. There were more orders than prints. I suggested that Dave do another piece in the same vein, and he came up with *Misty Morning — Ruffed Grouse.* It's similar in structure to the woodcock painting and has that same early morning, October atmosphere. We increased the edition size for this one to 575 copies, and they sold out, too, even faster than the other."

Exploring variations within a basic theme was hardly a new idea, neither in music, literature, nor the graphic arts, but no one had tried it with limited-edition wildlife prints until Webster and Maass decided to expand the misty-morning paintings into a full series. Success followed success, with mallards, bobwhite quail, wood ducks, and green-winged teal. Advance orders for the last two claimed every print before the paintings were finished, and both David Maass and Wild Wings discovered an approach that remains successful today.

"I enjoy working with the serial concept," Dave says. "It gives me an opportunity to explore the subtle differences inherent to certain kinds of similar experience. Obviously a lot of different birds have to cope with the same weather, and I'm interested in how they behave and how they look in those conditions, whether it's a damp, hazy fall day or a cold morning after a snowstorm or some other situation. By setting up a consistent condition through several paintings, I can focus on the birds themselves and how each species demonstrates its individuality. I'm interested, too, in how different environments appear in similar weathers."

The *Misty Morning* series also demonstrates a key element in the breadth of David Maass' appeal. The damp, misty chill of the morning woods strikes a familiar note in every bird hunter's memory. We've all known those days, just after leaf-fall, when autumn is at a perfect balance between Indian summer past and winter yet to come, and if there's a hunter who doesn't have at least one especially fine memory of a day like that, I have yet to meet him.

But even if a Maass scene looks most familiar to a hunter, it appeals to the non-hunter as well. Anyone interested in wildlife and the outdoors can appreciate the world through David Maass' eyes.

Now, after 150 published prints totaling more than 80,000 copies, David Maass has become a principal member

Top: Bill Webster, founder of Wild Wings and now the company's chief executive officer. Above: Misty Morning–Ruffed Grouse, *second in the history-making series of game bird prints.*

of Wild Wings' stable, a group that includes many of the finest wildlife artists in the world. Counting duck stamp and conservation prints and fine-art pieces published by other houses, signed David Maass prints now number almost 140 editions, with more than 215,000 copies altogether. Only a handful of artists are more widely published. In sheer numbers, however, the fine-art prints scarcely hold a candle to the calendar reproductions, which by now total more than 21 million.

"Calendar art" typically has been the province of second-rate material indifferently printed, comprising lifeless landscapes, maudlin images of children and small pets, or mildly prurient

cheesecake presented under titles as self-consciously mock-aesthetic as "Moon Glow" or as locker-room ribald as "Reaching for the Soap." Until fairly recently, not many calendar companies went to the trouble or the expense of seeking out serious art, and even fewer insisted that their printers maintain high standards of quality in matching the color and density of the originals.

Brown & Bigelow of St. Paul, one of the oldest and largest calendar companies in the United States, is a notable exception, particularly with wildlife art. The company's Wilderness Wings calendar, which features game birds, has been an extremely popular item for many years, and for many years it primarily was the work of Richard Bishop, who was among the first modern generation of great American wildlife artists and designer of the 1936 federal duck stamp. Then came David Maass.

"In the late '50s, one of my colleagues at Josten's was a former Brown & Bigelow staff artist, and he suggested that I submit some paintings for possible calendar prints. I showed some to Clair Fry, who was their art director. He was very nice about it, but the bottom line was that Brown & Bigelow had Richard Bishop and didn't really need any more wildlife art."

But in the early '70s, when Bishop announced his retirement, Clair Fry still remembered David Maass.

"Clair himself was about to retire then, but he called and asked if I was still interested in painting for Brown & Bigelow. I went up to St. Paul and met with him and some other executives, and the short version of the story is that I delivered my twentieth set of paintings to

Peaceful Pair–Mallards appeared on the 1973 issue of Brown & Bigelow's "Wilderness Wings" calendar. Maass has been creating B&B calendar images since 1972.

Brown & Bigelow about two weeks ago. They're for the 1991 calendar.

"I suppose some artists might turn up their noses at the idea of painting for calendars, but it's an attitude that's never made much sense to me, especially when you're talking about a company like Brown & Bigelow, which has always done an excellent job in reproducing art. Besides, a good painting is a good painting, no matter what it's for, and I've won several awards with paintings I've done for their calendars.

"Actually, Brown & Bigelow has given me an opportunity to paint some things that I might not have done otherwise. At first, I did seven paintings each year for them, six each year since 1983; we discuss what species of birds to do, but otherwise they've always given me a completely free hand to design the paintings any way I want."

The fine-art phenomenon continued to blossom through the 1970s and '80s. By the late '70s, Wild Wings was distributing well over a million catalogues each year, and it was not uncommon for a new Maass print to sell out on the strength of its pre-publication announcement.

"Not many artists are as consistently good as Dave," Bill Webster says. "Every bird he paints is correct and appealing, and people learned long ago that they could depend on that."

Fine-art prints and calendar work were more than enough to ensure lasting success, but yet another field has bloomed for David Maass.

Although their present significance in the world of wildlife art has developed largely within the past twenty years, wildlife stamps are nothing new. The concept originated in the dustbowl-and-Depression days of the early 1930s, devised as a means by which the federal government could raise money in aid of a rapidly dwindling wildfowl resource. With the Migratory Bird Act, Congress authorized the government to collect a special annual fee from waterfowl hunters and stipulated that the net revenue be spent on preserving and enhancing wetland habitat.

Since a fee requires a receipt, someone came up with the notion of issuing a stamp that could be pasted onto a hunting permit as evidence of payment. Cartoonist and conservation activist Ding Darling designed the first such stamp, which was issued in 1934, and the rest, as they say, is history, since the migratory bird stamp remains a key source of funding for waterfowl conservation at the federal level.

The stamp took on some artistic significance almost immediately. The government never has paid for stamp designs, not even in the program's early days, before designs were chosen by competition; artists instead have always donated their work to the conservation cause. But in return, the government claims ownership of the image only as a stamp, leaving the artists free to issue reproductions of the original paintings in any numbers they choose.

Although duck stamps arguably are the wellspring of today's thriving print

Few artists can match Maass' success in duck stamp competitions. From top: Winning 1974 federal design of wood ducks, working sketch for his 1983 Arkansas duck stamp (page 43), and 1952 design of ring-necked ducks, his first entry in the federal.

market, the torrent was a long time building. All of the federal duck-stamp designs have been published as prints (or, in the days of black-and-white duck stamps, as lithographs or etchings), but interest in wildlife art — particularly reproductions — was such that twenty-odd years passed before they created more than a ripple in the art world. Editions were minuscule by current standards; prints of the Ding Darling stamp, for instance, numbered only about 300. For many years Abercrombie & Fitch of New York maintained an unofficial monopoly on publishing federal duck stamp prints, issuing them in editions of 250 copies that sold for about $15 each.

The trend toward larger editions of more expensive prints began about 1956, but even by the early 1970s, press runs averaged only about 1,000 copies and selling prices only about $60 per print. The indirect value of winning the

federal stamp competition similarly had begun to increase, although equally slowly. At first, being able to claim a federal duck stamp was a nice item for an artist's resumé, but of little value otherwise. As the federal competition gained prestige, however, winning artists began to realize greater indirect returns through enhanced reputation, and increased sales of both prints and original work.

Now, of course, winning "the federal," as it's called in art circles, is the Big Casino, tantamount to winning an Oscar or the Grand American, hitting the lottery, sweeping the World Series, finishing No. 1 at Wimbledon, and finding the Grail — all wrapped into one. The stamp print, in astronomical numbers, is a certain sell-out, as are many of the artist's other works for some time to come. Time naturally will winnow out the flukes — and there have been some — but it's safe to say that a good artist who wins the federal these days can be assured of financial security for a lifetime.

For the most part, all of this has come to pass in less than twenty years, closely correlated with the print market's astonishing growth. The process has been more avalanche than evolution, and it started with David Maass.

"I started entering the federal competition in the 1950s, back when all the entries had to be in black and white. My pieces did pretty well; I took third-place one year and tied for first in 1963. I got second-place on the re-vote.

"I've generally managed to finish in the running over the years; I've come in third, tied for second, taken second-place outright — a good enough showing, all told, to keep my enthusiasm up. I didn't enter in '72 — had a bad case of pneumonia that year and missed the deadline."

T he brass ring came into grasp a year later with a painting of two wood ducks and the contest for the 1974 federal stamp.

"I was ecstatic when they called to tell me I'd won. My family was, too, naturally, and I can't tell you how good it made me feel to call my mother and Kelly with the news. Kelly had always been there for me, right from the beginning. He'd taken me hunting, taught me to shoot, encouraged me to paint. He couldn't have been more supportive. I always felt grateful for his help but never more so than right then."

After the first flush of excitement subsided there was the matter of the print to consider, and David Maass made a decision that would change the way duck-stamp prints were marketed.

"I believed then, and still believe, that limited editions ought to be just that — limited. Especially if it's to be a numbered edition. At the time, I'd never even considered going beyond about 600 copies, numbered or not, but Bill Webster and I talked it over, and I decided to let the demand determine the press run.

"I contacted all the wildlife art dealers (there weren't all that many, at the time) and established a deadline; the number of orders I received by a certain date would be the total run, however many that happened to be. Well, when the deadline passed, I had orders for 2,800 prints. That was almost three times larger than any duck-stamp print edition had ever been, but that was the demand, so I went with it. I didn't number them, though; I just couldn't see 2,800 prints as a limited edition."

Since then, every artist who has won the federal competition has followed David Maass' approach in establishing edition sizes; the 2,800 copies that once seemed outrageous now are only a fraction.

As stamp and print collecting began noticeably to enhance the federal program's already substantial success in generating conservation revenue, state governments recognized an opportunity to bolster their own shrinking coffers. California in 1971 was the first to establish a state waterfowl stamp, followed by Iowa in 1972. Forty-three states now have waterfowl-stamp

Minnesota artists, it seems, have a stranglehold on the federal duck stamp competition. From left are Phil Scholer, Les Kouba, Maass, Art Cook, Richard Plasschaert, and Harvey Sandstrom. Other Minnesota artists who have painted federal designs include Francis L. Jaques, 1940-41; Roger E. Preuss, 1949-50; Edward A. Morris, 1961-62 and 1962-63; and Dan Smith, 1988-89.

Maass and daughter Jenni in his former home-studio at Fish Lake. The photograph was for a Ducks Unlimited magazine article announcing his selection as DU's artist of the year for 1974.

programs, and some require hunters to purchase "habitat" stamps as well. Private organizations hitched onto the same bandwagon, offering stamps and prints in aid of a growing list of wildlife species.

For the most part, these programs have proven a boon both to wildlife conservation and to the art world. States typically have commissioned artwork for their first stamps and selected subsequent pieces through contests modeled after the federal competition. The state contests do not confer the same level of prestige as the federal, but they do offer young artists a toehold toward wider recognition, and winning designs by established artists often generate optimum revenue for conservation — essentially a profitable situation from either side.

Winning one or two or a half-dozen contests hardly forms a basis for intelligently evaluating an artist's work, but consistent, long-term success in the stamp-and-print milieu says something for his skill, his reputation, and sometimes — as in the case of David Maass — for the nature of the man himself.

The statistics alone are impressive. David Maass has so far designed twenty-eight waterfowl and conservation stamps and prints — for waterfowl, grouse, wild turkeys, and quail; for Minnesota, Arkansas, Texas, New York, Maine, New Jersey, Missouri, and North Dakota; for

Ducks Unlimited, the International Quail Foundation, the Ruffed Grouse Society, the National Wild Turkey Federation, the Delta Waterfowl Research Station, the Minnesota Wildlife Heritage Foundation, the Wildlife Legislative Fund of America, the short-lived Buzzard Council of America, and most recently, for the North American Waterfowl Management Plan.

And why? "Because it's something I can do for wildlife and for the organizations that are dedicated to conservation. Let's face it: We're not going to have a healthy environment nor healthy wildlife populations just by wishing. It takes effort and it takes money.

"All of the various organizations — DU, the Grouse Society, the Quail Foundation, the Turkey Federation, all of them — want essentially the same thing; they want to conserve wildlife by conserving habitat. I don't know of a better way to spend money than on wildlife habitat, but you can't spend what you don't have. The organizations have done a lot of fund-raising with artwork, both stamps and prints, and it's important that they have artwork to rely on. The work they do is important to me, and I'm happy to do what I can to help."

Considering that David Maass' duck-stamp and conservation prints together have accounted for more than 125,000 individual copies, the help has been substantial.

Over the past fifteen years, David Maass has been honored as Artist of the Year by virtually every conservation organization in America. Ducks Unlimited, probably the greatest beneficiary of Maass' interest in conservation, has done so twice, naming him DU Artist of the Year in 1974 and as DU's first International Artist of the Year in 1988.

"Everyone has a favorite cause, and waterfowl is mine. Ducks are my specialty, so to speak, both as an artist and a hunter. I've done quite a few pieces for Ducks Unlimited to use as fund-raisers, and it pleases me that DU has been able to use them successfully.

"It's my way of sharing the success I've been fortunate enough to have, my way of giving something back to the wildlife and the land."

Beyond their economic value, conservation stamps have created an artistic sub-genre, and David Maass is one of the master practitioners.

"The main problem with a stamp, obviously, is the size. Doing a painting is one thing, but shrinking it down to a couple of square inches is another thing altogether. Whatever you do has to be bold and it has to be simple; details just get lost in a format that small.

"Stamps are more design that art, and I was a designer before I was an artist. Maybe that's given me an edge. In any case, I work for a simple, strong shape when I'm designing a stamp. I keep the main subject quite large. If there are two birds, I'll keep both of them about the same size and headed the same direction, probably overlap them for unity.

"When the thing is reduced to stamp size, the viewer should be able to instantly recognize the birds and know what they're doing. This principle is all the more important if you set out to win a stamp competition, since that's presumably what the judges are looking for.

"Competition is something of a game, trying to guess what's going to catch the judges' eyes. They're looking at hundreds of entries, pretty much all at the same time, and you have to find something that will stand out from all the rest.

"I've found, though, that trying to anticipate the judges really isn't the way to go. I've had better success when I

Top: Working sketch of a wild turkey for Monarchs of the Hardwoods *(page 164). Above: Maass and Bill Webster with President Jimmy Carter in the Oval Office, where they presented him with print number one of* Monarchs of the Hardwoods. *The edition was published in 1980 by the National Wild Turkey Federation.*

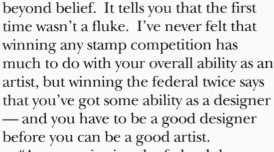

Top: 1982 Migratory Bird Hunting Stamp (page 169). Above, Maass and noted outdoor writer Gene Hill became friends while collaborating on their 1978 book, A Gallery of Waterfowl and Upland Birds.

simply focus on creating the strongest design I can. There's always the element of chance, but that's what makes competitions fun. And gratifying when you win.

"I'm always flattered when a state or an organization commissions me to design a stamp, but I get a bigger kick out of winning a juried contest; then I know it's the piece itself that's won, not my reputation.

"That's how I felt when I won the federal the second time."

With good reason. In 1982, 2,099 artists entered the federal, the largest number in the program's history. Among them all, the judges liked a piece that showed three canvasbacks bulling their way through the wind. They could have found virtually the same three birds in a David Maass painting called *Sweeping the Narrows.*

"I always liked those three ducks. They made a really strong center of interest in *Sweeping the Narrows,* and I decided to use them again as my entry in the federal and see if anyone else thought they were as powerful an image as I did. Apparently so.

"It's a great thrill to win the federal at all, but winning twice is gratifying beyond belief. It tells you that the first time wasn't a fluke. I've never felt that winning any stamp competition has much to do with your overall ability as an artist, but winning the federal twice says that you've got some ability as a designer — and you have to be a good designer before you can be a good artist.

"Anyway, winning the federal the second time was a tremendous kick. My first wife, Kim, and I had been divorced for a few years by then, and I was about to blow up, wanting to tell somebody. Mom and Kelly and Jenni and her husband Al were as excited as I was, and I was going to take them all out to dinner to celebrate. Then I remembered I had a date — with Gene Hill.

"Gene and I had collaborated on a book for Petersen Publishing Company, called *A Gallery of Waterfowl and Upland Birds,* and had become friends. He was in St. Paul on some business, and we'd planned to have dinner together that evening.

"I was in such a state after the call from Washington that I probably shouldn't have driven up to St. Paul. I did, but I sure don't remember much about the trip."

Gene Hill: "For a while, it was like having dinner with a zombie. Dave was almost in shock, although I don't know why he was so surprised. It didn't surprise me, anyway, but then I always have thought he's one of the greatest wildlife painters who ever lived.

"Anyway, we managed to celebrate the occasion properly — except for champagne. We tried to order some, but the restaurant didn't have any. Next time you talk to Dave, tell him he still owes me a bottle."

A lot of waterfowl, ducks and geese alike, use Lake Minnetonka, either as a stopover or as a place to spend the summer. There are some extremely interesting places to paint here, even though houses occupy much of the lakeshore.

I wanted to emphasize the mass and power of these birds, so I showed them coming in, legs down, wings cupped, tails fanned, looking about as large as they can. They're so big and strong that even a small flock is an impressive sight.

Rest Site — Canada Geese,
Oil, 26 x 38, 1987 (© Brown & Bigelow, 1989)

I have used landscapes near home in many paintings, wherever home happened to be at the time. This one is a view of Lake Minnetonka, just down the bay from our house. The old barn and water tower are landmarks on Maxwell Bay; the first time I saw the scene, I thought it would be a great background for a painting. We see it in all moods, from bright sunshine to fog to snow — in every season.

I decided to paint it as the shore looks in late fall, when most of the leaves are down, and that's a time when a lot of diving ducks gather on the lake. I really like working with the light and shadow that I see during the fall, especially just after a storm, when the heavy weather is breaking up and some sunlight is starting to come through.

We see a lot of buffleheads on Minnetonka, often flying very low, almost as if they're running across the waves. They're busy little ducks; they drop into some spot, stay a while, get up, circle the bay, and come down somewhere else. Great fun to watch.

Autumn Flight — Buffleheads
(formerly Lifting Weather),
Oil, 24 x 32, 1989 (© Brown & Bigelow, 1991)

B ill Webster commissioned this painting almost thirty years ago, not long after I first met him. We got to know one another quite well while I was working on this piece, and we've been friends ever since.

Bill wanted a painting of canvasbacks and wanted the setting to be the upper end of Lake Pepin, just down the hill from his house. The 26-mile-long lake was created by a dam on the Mississippi River, which at this point forms the Minnesota-Wisconsin border. Here, you're looking across the lake from the Minnesota side toward the scenic bluffs on the Wisconsin side. Canvasbacks travel this route during the migration; in fact, the Upper Mississippi National Wildlife Refuge attracts almost 90 percent of the flyway's canvasbacks each fall.

Reserve Bay — Canvasbacks,
Oil, 24 x 36, 1963

I don't often paint songbirds, but the colors in these trees are so subdued that I thought it would be interesting to work with bright birds for contrast. Cardinals struck me as perfect subjects. Even so, I was careful to keep my palette toned down, so I wouldn't overpaint them.

A New Day—Cardinals,
Oil, 26 x 21, 1987

I n 1983 the Minnesota chapter of the National Wild Turkey Federation asked me to design the first Minnesota turkey stamp. As with other stamps, the purpose was to raise money for habitat and to promote turkey conservation.

I chose the Whitewater Valley in southeastern Minnesota as the setting, for several reasons. For one, it's where the Minnesota biologists released the first birds in their turkey restoration program.

Besides that, the Whitewater Valley has some personal significance. My uncle was the first park ranger at Whitewater State Park, which is next to what now is Whitewater Wildlife Refuge, one of the largest wildlife management areas in the state. I used to spend summers there when I was a kid, and I got to know it quite well. It's been fascinating to see the changes that have taken place there just in my lifetime, and I've used the area several times in paintings.

The iridescence in the turkey's plumage is difficult to capture, almost a trial-and-error process until you get it right. There's no particular formula that I know of, but I probably mix more color for painting a turkey than for any other bird.

You can use lots of bright colors, but you have to use them in ways that don't lead the viewer to think the feathers actually are those colors. That sounds contradictory, but the fact is, iridescence changes color as the angle of light changes. As I have the birds standing here, the feathers show certain colors, but if the birds were turned a bit or if the angle of the sun changed even slightly, then the colors would be different.

Whitewater Valley Gobblers,
Oil, 13 x 18, 1983

This probably has more personal significance than any mallard painting I've done. It was selected as the first Ducks Unlimited International Artist of the Year print.

The setting is Arnold Krueger's place in southern Minnesota, where he and I have opened a lot of duck seasons together, and in fact, I had opening day in mind when I did the piece. My intention was to combine changing colors — the mixture of autumn colors and fading summer green — with unsettled, changing weather. Changing seasons, in other words. This weather could go either way; it could turn into a bluebird day if the clouds broke up, or they might thicken and bring some rain or snow. That's opening day for you.

Greenhead Alert,
Oil, 24 x 36, 1987

This is the second painting in the *Flyway* series. I wanted a distinctively West Coast background, but not any specific place. This could be the Sacramento Valley, but it also could be any one of a hundred other places.

The Flyway concept is particularly strong in the composition of this painting. By creating a structural tension between the mountain range and the layered sky, Maass draws the viewer deeply into the background, thereby suggesting vast distance. His arrangement of the birds is another flyway metaphor; showing the ducks funneling down toward the foreground suggests, in miniature, the similar pattern by which waterfowl move on a continental scale through each of the flyways.

Pintails — Pacific Flyway,
Oil, 28 x 24, 1987

I entered a painting almost identical to this in the 1978 federal duck stamp competition and came in third. I liked the design, so I thought I'd try something similar for the Minnesota contest. It became my second Minnesota state stamp.

In a juried stamp contest, the key for me has been to concentrate on design, to work at getting the most pleasing composition using just two or three birds and the simplest kind of background.

1979 Minnesota Waterfowl
Stamp — Pintails, Oil, 13 x 18, 1978

*S*ince I think of swans in terms of vast spaces, I decided to place this flock against open sky. It was something like working on a stamp painting, certainly in the sense that it's quite simple and also because design is such a vital element. I arranged the clouds both to lend a sense of great depth and space, and also to complement the pattern of the birds.

Lofty Altitudes — Whistling Swans,
Oil, 24 x 32, 1986 (© Brown & Bigelow, 1988)

*S*ince this was to be a stamp, I naturally wanted primary emphasis to be on the bird itself, but I also wanted a hint of the kind of habitat that woodcock need. Woodcock habitat is usually quite dense; but how do you show that without making the painting too busy to be an effective stamp design? I chose to suggest thick vegetation at the bottom and fairly dense woods in the background, hazed out enough that it doesn't compete with the main subject.

Perhaps more than some others, woodcock are birds that you really need to see in the wild if you want to paint them accurately. Just looking at pictures, for instance, you might assume that they fly with their bills pointing forward, the way most birds do. But they don't; they seem to carry their bills at about a forty-five-degree angle downward, no matter what attitude of flight they are in. They have to, because their eyes are on top of their heads.

1987 Ruffed Grouse Society
Stamp — Woodcock,
Oil, 13 1/2 x 18 1/2, 1986

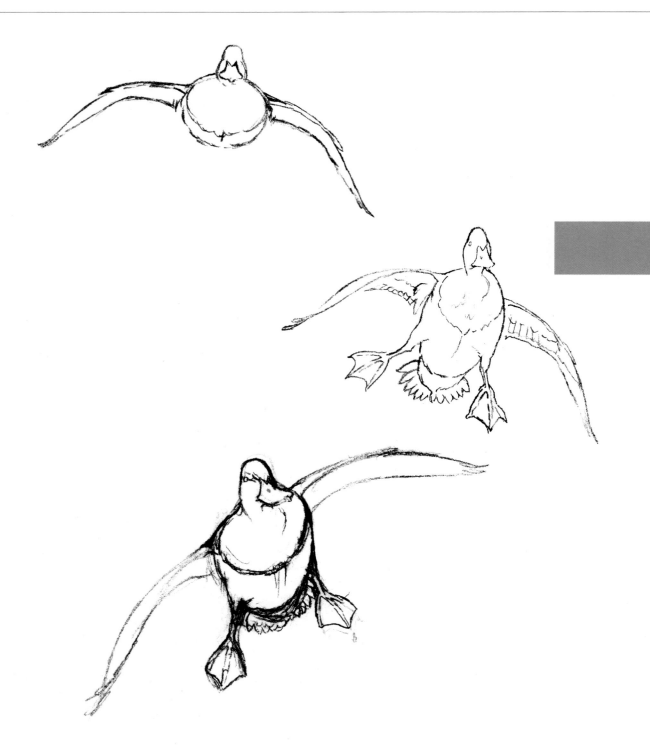

O f all my paintings, this is one of my favorites, partly because it relates so closely to Jimmy Robinson.

The first time I hunted with Jimmy on the Delta Marsh in Manitoba, he and I and Frank Lavalle went out to a place the guides had named Jimmy's Point. It was a great spot for bluebills, although a lot of canvasbacks and even some puddle ducks came in there, too.

Hunting divers, especially bluebills, over decoys in big water is a tremendous thrill, and the birds kept flying throughout the morning. We took our limits right away and then just sat and watched. There were flocks of birds in the distance, just as I have them here, and lots of ducks that worked in over the decoys. A few came down, but most flared off at the last moment, as soon as they realized that someone was in the blind. I never look at this painting without thinking about Jimmy and the good times we spent together.

Jimmy's Point — Bluebills,
Oil, 24 x 36, 1981

This is one of the most recent paintings of any in this book. I did it after a hunting trip in Arkansas in December '88.

Hunting in the green-timber reservoirs of Arkansas is exciting. The birds circle and circle over the trees, in flocks from twenty-five to five hundred. They work lower and lower, while everyone calls like mad, and each time they come around, you think, "This is it." Sometimes they go on circling, and sometimes they just leave. But when they do set their wings and come down, it's incredible. Often we just let them come in and sit on the water until something spooks them, and then watch them rise and fly off, without firing a shot.

One thing I really like about the Arkansas clubs where I hunt is that nobody shoots hens. Considering what's happening to duck populations these days, it's an important conservation measure.

Green Timber — Mallards,
Oil, 24 x 36, 1989

I did an earlier Texas duck stamp and used wood ducks, only two birds and presented quite large. Martin Wood, who owns Collector's Covey in Dallas and who publishes the Texas duck stamps, suggested a different approach for this one.

His idea was to do something unlike the typical stamp—more like a miniature painting complete with an environment that was recognizably Texan. This has more birds than most of my other stamp designs, and they aren't as large, but it seems to work well.

1989 Texas Duck Stamp — Mallards,
Oil, 13 x 18, 1988

I was thinking of the northern prairies when I designed this scene, possibly Saskatchewan, with the big wheatfields and grain elevators and that enormous sky. It's truly snow goose country, hence the flocks in the far distance.

I wanted to get some really dark values in the sky and contrast those with cloud shadows on the wheat. The dark sky, of course, lets the white geese stand out. Putting a white bird against a pale sky isn't nearly as dramatic.

Migrating Flight — Snow Geese,
Oil, 24 x 32, 1988 (© Brown & Bigelow, 1990)

W *ildlife on the cusp between man's influence and that of nature is a familiar theme in David Maass' art. Whether the subject is grouse in an abandoned orchard or waterfowl in farmlands, Maass often explores the borders where man and nature meet.*

Here, both influences are clear. This lake margin once was dry land, as the now-derelict fenceline shows. At some earlier time, cattle may have been the only animals one might see in this place, but now, as nature asserts its own influence, these bluewings tell us that what we often see as wasteland embodies a significance and a beauty all its own.

Alarmed — Blue-Winged Teal,
Oil, 24 x 32, 1977 (© Brown & Bigelow, 1979)

When I think of wild turkeys in Minnesota, I always think of the Whitewater Valley. After repeated attempts to stock pen-raised birds in the Whitewater, the then Minnesota Department of Conservation decided to release some wild turkeys brought in from Missouri. These birds, interestingly, were obtained in a trade for walleye fingerlings from Minnesota hatcheries. From that small flock of Missouri birds introduced in the 1950s, Minnesota's wild turkey population has expanded into several neighboring counties.

The Whitewater, by the way, is a painter's paradise, loaded with rocks, extremely hilly, and with lots of birch and aspen and hardwoods.

Strolling Gobblers — Eastern Wild Turkeys, Oil, 24 x 32, 1989 (© Brown & Bigelow, 1991)

A wood duck drake is a bright autumn day in the form of a bird, and this painting demonstrates David Maass' splendid ability to devise a mutual interplay of subject and environment. Somewhere in the background–in the vibrant blue sky, in the clouds, the vegetation, or in the slight color shift of objects reflected in the water–you can find an echo of every tone and value in the ducks' plumage. As in virtually every Maass painting, these birds in this place at this time present an irreducible unity.

In the hands of a less skillful artist, so much sheer brightness could easily become a caricature, but Maass has chosen instead to contrast the more colorful aspects of his subjects with other, less dramatic details. This is particularly apparent in the two foreground drakes, only one of which shows the full range of colors typical of their plumage. The other birds, the intensity of their values reduced by natural coloration or distance, offer additional balance against the brightest tones of both the birds and the background.

Autumn Shades — Wood Ducks,
Oil, 24 x 36, 1988

W inter is a rough time for quail all across the northern part of their range, and I guess that was in the back of my mind when I designed this piece. The other *Early Winter Morning* paintings show fairly "pretty" landscapes, but I don't imagine that many people would see much beauty in this setting.

Actually, it's a little ravine not far from my house on Fish Lake, full of willows and stumps and broken-down trees. It's the kind of place that looks good to a covey of quail, especially at that time of year, which can be pretty desolate. That's why I chose it, to suggest that if we're going to conserve wildlife, we need to make sure that such places are there for the birds to use.

Early Winter Morning — Bobwhites,
Oil, 36 x 30, 1981

I wanted to paint some waterfowl in a typical East Coast setting. I chose canvasbacks because they're a classic Eastern Seaboard duck. The setting is Rhode Island Sound, right at the mouth of Narragansett Bay; that's the Beaver Tail Light in the background, one of the most famous lighthouses in New England.

Lighthouse Point — Canvasbacks,
Oil, 13 x 18, 1989

(Following page)

*T*o puddle ducks, a haven can be a modest swatch of landscape. Slough or pothole, marshy creek bottom or pond–almost any bit of water with protective vegetation nearby offers the sort of habitat these birds need for survival. Such habitat is less spectacular than the broad expanses of open water that diving ducks prefer, and it's more easily spent. The long-time and widespread practice of draining small wetlands has had a profound and unhappy impact upon North American waterfowl.

As in many Maass paintings, there is subtle poignancy in Disturbed Haven, *derived in this case from the contrast between foreground and background. By juxtaposing waterfowl habitat and agriculture, the painting poses questions: Will this bit of marsh survive or be swallowed up in land use practices that leave fewer and fewer havens for wildlife? Will foreground and background one day become indistinguishable?*

The painting itself offers no predictions, only a view of what might be lost.

Disturbed Haven — Widgeon,
Oil, 24 x 32, 1982

A WORLD THROUGH THE HUNTER'S EYES

David Maass works in a log cabin that stands at the edge of the woods, a short distance from the house. It smells of coffee and oil paint and the faint tang of turpentine.

"The cabin was here when we bought the land a few years ago, about the time Ann and I were married. It was standing right where we wanted to build the house, but it was such a solid little thing that we decided to have it moved and remodeled as a studio. It's a good place to work."

An understatement. It looks like a splendid place to work, comfortable as a hunting lodge, snug as a burrow. For anyone who works at home, it's the stuff of fantasy — a little kitchen for refueling the coffee, an office, and a long, airy room with a north wall that's mostly glass. Plenty of space for an easel, a drawing table, storage cabinets, space for books, space for files, for prints and photos on the walls, for all the clutter of little things that spark private memories.

An artist's workspace has an air of magic about it — or so it seems to me, possibly because semi-legible handwriting is the full extent of my graphic talent. There is magic, too, in the process by which people create products of the imagination, and the various means of approach is a favorite topic of conversation among those who do such work. No matter if they're artists, writers, composers, or what, get two or three professionals in the same room for more than half an hour, and they'll end up trading descriptions of their working habits and their particular approaches, end up talking shop.

A David Maass painting begins on the drawing table: "I try to plan things out as thoroughly as possible. The more I know about a piece before I start painting, the better it goes. It's easy to get lost if I don't have a clear sense of what I'm trying to achieve and how I intend going about it.

"Even so, there's no such thing as a perfectly planned painting, at least not in my case. There always are some things that simply evolve as I'm working, some things that seem to work out different — and usually better — from the way I've planned.

"The one thing that almost never changes, though, is composition. When I finish a painting that has several birds in it, they'll be right where I put them in the beginning. That's basic structure, and it won't work unless you stick to it — like building a house and deciding halfway through to change the foundation or the frame. If I get into a painting and decide that I have to change one of the main-subject birds, then I'll just scrap it and start over. Faulty composition isn't something that tinkering after the fact is going to cure.

"Now, that's not to say I won't paint out some background birds or add a few. If I do, it's usually a matter of accommodating something that's evolved as I've done the painting. But all in all, the more pencil work I do in the beginning, the less monkeying around I have to do once I start putting the paint down."

What emerges when David Maass begins putting the paint down is a style of art usually described as realistic, an assessment that strikes me as partly accurate, partly misleading. *Authentic* seems to me a better word for images that are profoundly real without being tediously realistic, and in the distinction lies the heart of David Maass' approach to art.

"My intention is not to paint portraits of gamebirds but rather to present them as a hunter might see them, and I rely on my own experience as the guide to what I paint. That applies to every aspect of my work.

"I can't imagine any serious painter not using a camera for reference work. I certainly do, and there may be bits and

Dave Maass outside and inside his log cabin studio. Rustic yet functional, Maass' studio provides ample lighting and workspace, reflecting the artist's concern for thoughtful planning and organization. Photographs on these pages by Steve Peck, St. Paul, Minnesota.

pieces of a dozen photos in a single painting — but that doesn't mean I sit at the easel and copy them.

"Think of it this way: The camera records exactly what it sees, but it only sees for a fraction of a second. Suppose you have a camera with a motor drive and shoot a whole roll of film of some action, say, a flock of ducks coming in to land. Since you're recording tiny slices of that action, a whole series of them, it's possible that every frame will show extremely awkward postures. You could paint it that way, and it'd be real, but it wouldn't necessarily *look* real, simply because you're painting a transitional moment between one posture and another.

"That's where experience becomes vital. If you've never actually seen very many ducks in the air, you're likely to accept what the camera shows you. You may do the painting with perfect technique, but it won't look right to a viewer who's seen a lot of birds. I depend on my camera for reference material, but I seldom paint birds from photos.

"I rarely use mounted specimens, either, for the same reason. It's not that taxidermists can't do extremely accurate work, but I prefer to rely on my own eye and my own experience in designing the postures. Then, if it comes out wrong, it's nobody's fault but mine.

If I need to refresh my memory of a bird's plumage or if I'm painting a bird I'm less familiar with, a museum-type study skin works beautifully.

"Birds are challenging to paint, for several reasons. Plumage is always interesting, even among the more nondescript species. Those with really intricate markings — like grouse and woodcock and quail and such — are a delight to work with. But part of the challenge is in exercising judgement. The amount of detail I put into painting plumage depends on how close the bird is to the foreground, but even then I try to be careful about going too far with details. I can get bogged down in painting every feather and lose touch with what's going on in the image as a whole. And if I do that, I'm inviting the viewer to do the same thing.

"Since I try to show birds as you would see them in the wild, that usually means they're in flight. When you see a flying bird, you don't see every detail of its feathers; you see enough to recognize the bird, but you're at least as aware of what it's doing as you are of what it looks like. That's the balance I always try to maintain.

"On the other hand, what plumage I do show has to be accurate and believable. If it isn't, then I'm distracting the viewer in yet another way, taking him out of the action of the painting, and I don't want to do that."

*P*erhaps because I neither draw nor paint, I find the technical aspects of art endlessly mystifying.

Which isn't to say that art itself baffles me. I fancy that I can take a reasonably

clear-headed view of a piece once it's finished, but put me anywhere near someone of talent who has a pencil or brush in his hand, and my capacity for critical thought flies the coop. I'm the guy you'll find standing for hours next to some hack doing pastel portraits in a shopping mall, gawking like a farm boy at a fashion salon. I've pestered every artist I know with the same dumb question, applied to nearly everything you might find in a painting: How do you *do* that?

My friends, bless them, have always had the patient kindness to give me serious answers, even though the question must at times seem impossibly naive. I don't ask because I have any notion of trying it myself, but rather simply because the ability to draw and paint — to create a lifelike illusion of three-dimensional reality out of lifeless material on a two-dimensional ground — blows me away. It's mysterious and beautiful and mystical and meretricious — and even at the most mechanical levels it's all utter wizardry to me.

So how does David Maass do what he does?

"I paint primarily on presswood — masonite, if you care to call it that. You can buy presswood panels already prepared, but I've always done my own. It's a tricky process, but the result is a strong binding for the paint. It also protects the painting almost indefinitely against cracking.

"I start by giving the panel a glue size, using rabbit-skin glue, and sand it lightly once it's dry. Then it gets a layer of gesso, which is a dry powder. You mix it with water, let it set for a while, heat it, and put in onto the presswood. I like to thin the gesso down quite a bit and put on three or four coats, enough to make a pure white surface with none of the brown presswood showing through.

"When that's dry, I transfer my layout, which I've drawn on tracing paper, onto the gessoed panel in pencil. When the drawing is done — and it's usually fairly detailed — I size the panel again, using one thin coat of an acrylic matte medium. When that's dry, the surface is ready for paint.

"The matte medium serves two purposes. It seals the gesso so that it isn't too absorbent, and it also seals the pencil lines so the graphite doesn't float off and mix with the paint. I used to do the sizing with Damar varnish thinned with turpentine, but the surface was inconsistent. In some areas, the gesso would suck up paint like a sandbar, and that would cause problems. If I want a certain texture of some softness in a particular place, I prefer to do it with the brush.

"My approach to handling the paint is pretty straightforward — I put it on and work it until I'm satisfied with the way it looks. I put the paint on fairly heavily, too, and I like to work wet on wet. Consequently, I like to work as quickly as I can, get the background done and the birds in before any of it dries very much. The longer I have to leave something, the less satisfying the results are; when some areas start drying, it's more difficult keeping everything as soft as I like.

"I use sable brushes, as wide as I can get, especially on backgrounds. They're like chisels, wide in one dimension but thin the other way. I can work a lot of paint with them and do most of the fine

The Maass family in late 1989.
Top: Daughter Jenni and her husband,
Alan Doyle. Above: Dave with Paul, Ann,
and Kiska, a Siberian Husky and Pulse,
the family cat.

Maass works almost exclusively in oils and prefers to keep his colors natural and subdued.

work with the edge. About the only time I use smaller brushes is on the main subjects and sometimes in the foreground, where details need to be a bit finer. Otherwise, I want the biggest brush I can get.

"I almost always work from back to front — from background to foreground— and from top to bottom, starting with the sky and working down to the horizon line or to ground-level.

"Once the setting is done, with all the trees and foreground vegetation in, then I do the birds, starting with the ones farthest back, if there's a flock, and working forward. The main subjects are the last things I paint. If there are some very small background birds, I might paint them over paint I've already put down, but I rarely do that with the principal subjects. If you saw one of my paintings just at the last stage, you'd see a complete piece except for the birds; there you'd see unpainted gesso and birds drawn in pencil.

"I do it that way for a couple of reasons. For one, I lose my pencil lines if I paint over everything, and it's hard to go back in and put the birds exactly where I had them in the first place. I spend a lot of time drawing and work

hard at getting the composition the way I want it, and I want to be able to paint it exactly the way I drew it. Some artists do paint birds directly over their backgrounds. It seems to work for them, but it's never worked for me.

"I also believe I can get more vibrant color in the birds if I paint them on gesso instead of on other paint. Which isn't to say that I work in bright color; generally I don't. I used brighter colors years ago, when I first started painting for Brown & Bigelow, for instance. Dick Bishop, my predecessor, did very colorful work, and I used a palette similar to his for a while, until I worked out my own approach. Stu Ferreira used to caution me to keep my colors grayed down, keep them subdued. He was right."

Panels, pencils, brushes, and paint are an artist's tools, and he manipulates them into the imagery by which he communicates. They are, in a writer's terms, his paper and ink, the brushstrokes his vocabulary. The artist's language, however, is light.

In all but the most abstract of styles, light is the element that brings art truly alive. Light creates fullness out of form, lends vitality to geometric illusion. In light lies magic, and in David Maass' work, the magic sings.

"Each angle of light has its own particular challenge," Dave said, handing me a four-by-five transparency of a piece painted in 1987 for The Ruffed Grouse Society. I held it up toward the office window to see a single woodcock, frozen in mid-flush against a clump of white birch, the foreground scene washed in low-angle, morning light from the left side.

"When the sun is this low, you're going to have light on the undersides of some things in the picture, and that's tricky. So is the sideways angle, because you get strong highlights where the sun actually hits the subjects, but you also get reflected lights on the opposite side."

He points to the bird. "No sunlight is actually striking the bird's underside, but there's a lot of reflected light, which is cooler. The highlight is warm, with quite a bit of red in it, while the reflected light tends more toward greenish tinges.

"On the top wing, the light is so intense that the colors are almost entirely washed out. A woodcock's wing has a lot of color in it, but you don't see it when the light is particularly strong. The other wing is backlit and because the primary feathers are so thin, you see light coming through them. That's yet another challenge — showing less light where the feathers overlap and more translucence where they don't.

"Woodcock have sort of pinkish feet, but in light like this you wouldn't see them as all one color. Only where the light hits them directly do you get a sense of color. The rest is in shadow.

"It's the same with the trees. The strongest light is direct sun; the darkest area is right next to that, and then the intensity builds a bit as you come to the reflected-light side. Anyone looking at this would naturally say, 'That's a white birch,' but we don't actually see much of it as pure white, just the edge with the sun on it.

"It seems strange, but the trickiest part of painting a birch is getting it dark enough. I really work at that. You're dealing with a tree that's basically white, but the shadow side doesn't really look white to the eye. So, you have to paint that quite dark but still let the viewer know that it's a white tree — and also a round one.

"That's another problem with sidelight; it tends to make curved surfaces appear flat. In order to keep it round, you have to manipulate direct light against reflected light, with the deepest shadows in between.

"And then the branches ... tree branches grow in all directions, not just vertically and horizontally. So you have to find ways of showing branches coming toward the viewer and away from him. It's done entirely with the play of light; there's no other way, when you're only working in two actual dimensions. Any good artist can do it, of course, but you have to be thinking and seeing all the time to pull it off successfully."

He hands me another transparency, this one of a painting titled *Migrants — Pintails*. Here, a flock of eight sprig are settling in at a lakeshore edge under a lowering sky.

"When you paint birds against a sky like this, where you have dark, dense clouds in one area and lighter clouds with some open sky in another, you have to take different approaches to get what amounts to the same effect. The birds against the darkest part of the sky need to be strongly highlighted if they're to

The lifelike quality in this woodcock can be traced to the artist's use of light. "Each angle of light has its own particular challenge," says Maass while studying a transparency of this painting. The image was published as the 1987 Ruffed Grouse Society print.

stand out, but if you show other birds in the same flock against light sky, you have to do something different with the brush. The amount of sunlight actually is the same on all of them, but you have to tone down the highlights where there's less contrast. Otherwise, you can end up with something that looks like two different paintings.

"I always try to stay aware of the angle of light as I'm painting, and I usually work with something other than direct, overhead light. I like to work with some sunlight on the subject, even on cloudy days, so I don't often present the kind of completely overcast condition that makes everything look uniformly gray. Some artists can make that work extremely well, but I don't enjoy doing it. So, I try to break up the sky enough to get a little sunlight coming through. It adds interest for me, and of course, it helps direct the viewer's eye toward the main subject.

"I also use haze and mist quite a lot. It's an atmosphere that appeals to me strongly, both when I'm painting and when I'm outdoors. To accomplish that in a painting, I use less color in the background than I do in the mid- and foreground. I increase the values gradually as I work forward, getting more darks and more color, so that whatever is in the foreground has the most contrast — so that everything, in other

words, is the way you'd see it if you were there. The background fades out, which creates a sense of depth, and doesn't intrude on the subject.

"I don't do every painting that way, but it's wonderfully satisfying to create that particular mood. I suppose hazy backgrounds have become something of a trademark for me, which is okay. I love that sort of atmosphere, and it can be artistically sound besides. Fading intensity is one way our eyes perceive distance; the horizon isn't as intense as what's closest to us, no matter how bright the day is."

A waterfowl painter is also, by necessity, a painter of water, whether a lake surface, a marshland pool, or the shower of droplets from the feet and underbelly of a springing puddle duck.

On Dave's desk I spread out pictures of a half-dozen paintings, all showing water as a major element and all different, and ask, yet again, "How do you do that?"

Dave smiles. "The most elementary problem, but in many ways the most difficult one, is getting it to look like water instead of stone or concrete or aluminum foil or something else. The key is to do it as simply as I can: Put it down, work it until it looks wet, and then leave it alone.

"If there's a particularly dark sky, the water can take on very dark colors, depending on the light, and I have to remind myself of that quite often. I don't think I've ever finished that type of dark-day painting where I felt the water was too dark. If anything, I sometimes wish that I'd gone darker yet.

Hazy backgrounds, like this fog-enshrouded woods in Abandoned Orchard–Ruffed Grouse, *have become something of a trademark for Maass. Misty backdrops enhance the feeling of depth, while allowing the eye to focus on foreground subjects, which he paints with more contrast.*

  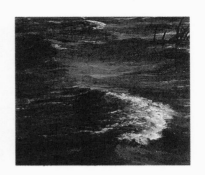

"The texture of water presents a set of demands all its own. Wind-whipped water looks one way, natural current or wave action looks another. Wind on deep water creates a texture different from wind on shallow water.

"This is one area where the camera is almost indispensable, just as it is for sky. I shoot a lot of reference photos of sky and water — just sky and water. I suppose the people at the photo lab think I'm some kind of lunatic, but those pictures are worth more than gold to me.

"Ice and water in the same painting can be tricky. If there are some trees and branches or rushes, you can help distinguish ice from water by showing shadows on the ice and reflections on the water. Ice has some texture, but it's basically flat; that and the lack of reflections are key differences. Snow helps, too, since snow obviously doesn't lie on water but does on ice.

"Otherwise, I use essentially the same palette for both. Perhaps I'll use a little more green in the ice, but the differences are subtle. After all, ice and water are the same thing in different forms. I don't give a lot of conscious thought to distinguishing the two; they look different, so I just paint them differently."

The day I arrived in Minnesota, Dave and I visited the American Museum of Wildlife Art in Old Frontenac, there to call on museum director Byron Webster. We spent a pleasant hour browsing through an exhibition of paintings by Francis Lee Jaques, one of the Old Masters of American wildlife art and a particular favorite for both of us. In one especially powerful canvas, Jaques shows a pair of buffleheads skimming the surface of calm water. The view is close up, above and slightly behind the birds, so that we see both their backs and, reflected in the water, their undersides — an immensely appealing treatment carried off with consummate mastery. I asked Dave later about the problems of painting reflections in water.

"Reflections are interesting to work with. How they look depends almost entirely on how still the water is. If it's perfectly still, you get almost a mirror image; you could turn the piece upside down and have trouble knowing which was which. That's so rare in nature, though, that it usually looks phony in a painting. I try to paint water with at least a slight ripple, which looks more natural and also helps make the water look wetter.

"The rougher the water, the more fragmented the reflections, of course, and really rough water scarcely reflects at all — or at least we scarcely see a reflection. What we do see actually is more shadow than reflection, and I can capture that with just a touch of color here and there. The hard part is getting them in the right places.

"If you shoot a photo of rough water and start analyzing it, you discover that it's amazingly intricate, with lots of lights and darks of various sizes. You have to be careful painting that sort of thing,

Details of three Maass paintings reveal the different moods of water: Glassy smooth, when surrounding vegetation is mirrored on the surface; rippled, when reflections become fragmented; and rough, with virtually no reflections but loaded with intricate lights and darks.

because you can work it to death, monkey with it to the point where it's so stiff that you lose any sense of movement.

"Painting reflections is like painting water itself: The less you fuss with it, the better the results."

If painting water goes with the territory of being a waterfowl painter, a Minnesota artist is obliged to paint a fair share of snow, and there's a particular skill in making it look like snow and not plaster of Paris or simply blobs of untempered white. Among David Maass' work, you'll find it in every form, from new-fallen fluff to the hard, grainy stuff of late winter.

A wildlife artist living in Minnesota must be comfortable with painting snow, whether it's freshly-fallen as in Frosty Stroll *(page 148) or the crusted version found just before spring.*

"Painting snow is also a lot like painting water. You have to be aware of getting the shadows intense enough. The brighter the day, the darker the shadows will be, and you need to add a lot of purple, blue, and gray values — and keep reminding yourself that it needs to be darker than you think.

"The actual color of snow depends on the values in the sunlight that's on it. On a bright day the snow takes on a warmer cast, and I use a certain amount of red. Things also tend to be redder early and late in the day. I look at my palette sometimes when I'm painting bright snow and think, 'That's too red.' But once I get it on the board and get the darks into the painting, then the snow looks white — warm, but white."

The realism of a typical David Maass painting is instantly available to even a cursory look. The images appear classically tight, the details specific and controlled — especially so if you're standing at a distance or seeing the piece reproduced in small size. Move in close, though, and you'll find a surprisingly loose, almost impressionistic approach. Stylistically, the difference between David Maass and the more obviously impressionistic painters resides more in degree than in kind.

The typical Maass original is a sizeable piece, perhaps two feet by three, and what from farther back appear to be finely rendered details become at arm's length a spirited tapestry of slashes and flicks and dabs and sweeps. Where you might expect tiny licks of pigment you'll find instead bold strokes. Some painters wield their brushes like cavalry sabers, others like scalpels; David Maass handles his with the deft, quick precision of a fencing foil.

Like its realism, the authenticity of a Maass painting is immediately apparent, but it works in a precisely opposite way. Instead of loosening away from realism on a closer look, as the style does, Maass' thematic content grows progressively more complex, more richly detailed, and more trenchant the longer you explore it. Each painting tells a story.

"What I'm after in nearly every painting is a presentation that puts the viewer into the scene. I seldom like to show a human being in the picture, but I almost always imply a presence. While I'm working on a piece, I imagine myself actually there and try to see everything as I would if I were hunting in that particular place, try to get a sense of the weather, the temperature — every part of the experience. Once it's done, then I can step out and let the viewer take my place."

Thematically, the implied human presence in a Maass painting is extremely important, for it creates a center, a specific point of view from which the whole narrative structure derives.

"I don't think you can do a successful painting that has more than one point of view. It just wouldn't look right.

"Take wind, for example. Wind obviously acts upon the environment — on water and trees and cattails, everything. Ducks respond to wind in specific ways. Wind direction relative to the viewer controls a lot of what should happen in the painting. If the viewer is on shore or in a blind at the edge of water and the wind is at his back, then the water in the foreground shouldn't be as rough as it is farther offshore, where there's no vegetation to protect it. But wind acts on shoreline vegetation about as strongly as it does on offshore water.

"If the wind is in the viewer's face, then the water will look different, and it's actually a bit easier to paint. With incoming wind, I can put the heavy waves in the foreground and create the perspective by making the waves smaller as distance increases. When the wind's blowing out, the waves actually get larger in the distance, but I have to paint them smaller in order to maintain the depth of the scene.

"Wind direction also affects the flight patterns of waterfowl. Ducks intending to land head into the wind, so the way I position the birds has to be consistent with the weather I've created. If the water and the vegetation show that wind

blowing straight at the viewer, I can't very well have the ducks facing him if they're coming in to land. I suppose that might not bother someone who hasn't seen many ducks, but a hunter would catch it instantly."

The birds themselves are the narrative heart of a David Maass painting and the element most unmistakably presented through a hunter's eyes. He seldom poses his birds but rather intercepts them for a moment as they have just arrived from somewhere and are on their way somewhere else. Whether it's a grouse captured a split-second before it flushes, a flock of turkeys picking their wary way through the woods, quail

Homeward Journey (page 76) depicts a flock of canvasbacks fighting a stiff autumn gale, just as the hunter might see them from his wind-swept blind.

135

Just as his stepfather introduced him to the outdoors, Dave Maass derives immense joy from hours afield with Paul. Top: Dave and Paul with Larry Grisham on a 1988 mallard hunt in Arkansas, and in 1987 at Delta Marsh.

huddled against the cold, or a flight of ducks winging the edges of a Minnesota lake, the lives of these birds clearly transcend the chronological limits of the paintings.

And here, too, that unseen human presence is vital. "I don't like to approach a scene as if there was no one within five miles of it. I'm interested in how birds behave when they're focused, when something has caught their attention and perhaps disturbed them a little. That's how I usually see them when I'm hunting. I think that's when they're at their best, and that's how I want to show them."

Jimmy's Point demonstrates both the intention and the success of David Maass' approach. Any casual look will find a flock of bluebills settling in at the edge of a lake. A hunter will see a great deal more than that. A hunter will recognize a wonderful tension among the ducks, will notice three distinctively different attitudes within the group, will know that there's a duckblind in this scene, out of sight in the foreground. Two birds are flaring off, four are all but

committed to land, and the rest are boring in toward the blind. A hunter will wonder what the flaring birds have seen that the others haven't and will wonder if those farther back will see the same thing. Every duck hunter knows that splendid moment of uncertainty. The flaring birds say it's the moment to stand and shoot; those in the background say it isn't.

"It's important to me to show the birds being themselves, doing what each species does that makes it unique. When I think of teal, for instance, I think of them zooming around, flying back and forth as if they just enjoy the exercise. Eiders seem to string out as they fly. Pintails, on the other hand, all come in at about the same time once they make up their minds to land somewhere. And they tend to come in at a bit steeper angle than some other ducks do, and tuck their tails more. Flushing woodcock always look as if they're surprised. That's the kind of realism I'm after, more than anything else."

A hunter can read fine old stories in David Maass' paintings, stories that stir memories grown sweet with time. One of my personal favorites, *Canyon Crossing — Ruffed Grouse,* takes me up to the birch woods on Olson's hill, a place in northern Minnesota that I've seen every year for nearly a quarter of my lifetime and hope to see during more autumns yet to come. *Misty Morning — Woodcock* moves me a mile or two south, into the coverts along the old Peterson road. It's a rare Maass piece that fails to take me somewhere, somewhere out in the weather, somewhere into a world on the cusp of winter, a world I'll always see through a hunter's eyes.

In the early 1960s I did quite a bit of photo research in the quail country of North Carolina. It's not at all unusual for me to use reference material compiled years earlier. I shoot a lot of pictures on research trips; some for immediate use, others which may stay in my files for many years before they are rediscovered and become part of a new painting.

The composition of this little covey is the result of observing hundreds of covey flushes. As for the birds themselves, I did what I usually do: I worked from study skins to get their markings and coloration.

Disturbed Bobwhites,
Oil, 24 x 32, 1987 (© Brown & Bigelow, 1989)

Maass

Wild Wings published prints from this painting, which were sold to help fund the Delta Research Station on the Delta Marsh in Manitoba. Delta's researchers have done some wonderfully valuable work on waterfowl breeding and feeding habits. Delta's efforts, coupled with Duck Unlimited's work on habitat and management, have contributed enormously to waterfowl conservation in North America.

Canvasbacks on the Delta Marsh,
Oil, 24 x 36, 1983

An interesting footnote to this painting can be seen in the two pintails at top. Several months after completing this piece, the thought occurred to me that the composition of those two birds would make a good duck stamp design — which is exactly what happened one year later when I recreated the pair for the 1979 Minnesota duck stamp.

Wary Descent — Pintails,
Oil, 24 x 32, 1978 (© Brown & Bigelow, 1980)

Ruffed grouse, they say, don't flush, they explode. And partridge, as they are called by hunters, don't just fly, they seem to almost scream through the trees. How they can maneuver through such dense foliage without colliding with a branch or tree is truly amazing.

So, how does the artist capture the birds in flight? It can be risky business not only to convey the bird authentically, but to recreate that electric moment when the birds erupt from the forest floor and vanish almost within seconds.

Through the Birches —Ruffed Grouse,
Oil, 24 x 32, 1986 (© Brown & Bigelow, 1987)

Part and parcel to the tremendous growth of wildlife art has been the appearance of many excellent shows and exhibitions. *Autumn Day —Woodcock* holds special significance to me, for it was one of several paintings that I exhibited at the first annual Minnesota Wildlife Heritage Foundation Art Show in Minneapolis. For years, it was the only wildlife art show in the country that was made up of artists from just one state. And it could only happen in Minnesota, which is considered by many as the home of the genre.

A month later, this painting was accepted for the prestigious Birds in Art Exhibition at Leigh Yawkey Woodson Art Museum in Wausau, Wisconsin. After that, it became part of a traveling exhibit that included the Smithsonian's National Museum of American Art in Washington, D.C.

Autumn Day — Woodcock,
Oil, 36 x 30, 1978

For its third stamp, the Maine Department of Inland Fisheries and Wildlife wanted wood ducks and asked me to indicate something of the conservation efforts that have gone into bringing back their numbers. Much of the restoration work, both in Maine and in other states as well, has involved providing habitat and nesting boxes, like those you see here.

Wood ducks are a bit tricky to paint, because it's easy to overdo their colors. They make popular subjects, since a lot of people consider them the most beautiful ducks of all.

Woodies are different from other ducks in ways that have nothing to do with coloration. When flying, the bird has a distinct silhouette with its short bill, somewhat long body, and squared-off tail.

1986 Maine Duck Stamp — Wood Ducks,
Oil, 6 x 9, 1986

This is the third painting in the *Flyway* series. As in the others, I wanted ducks and an environment typical of the area. This spot actually is not far from where I live, but you could find places just like it all the way down the Mississippi Flyway. And it certainly is classic wood duck habitat.

Although all the flyway paintings work on a common theme, this one is a bit different in that I didn't put any other birds in the far background. There is enough going on here, with all the trees, so that more birds would make things look too cluttered.

Mississippi Flyway — Wood Ducks,
Oil, 24 x 20, 1988

This is a patch of woods not far from where I lived in southern Minnesota. Not very picturesque, I'll admit, but I sometimes like to work with places that have no particular natural charm about them — dead branches lying around, tree trunks broken off, snarly weeds, the kind of place that wouldn't get a second look from a casual passerby. But if you put in some birds, it becomes the kind of place that would look great to a pheasant, or a pheasant hunter.

Frosty Stroll — Pheasants,
Oil, 24 x 32, 1986 (© Brown & Bigelow, 1988)

I enjoy painting waterfowl in rough-weather situations—not because waterfowl hunting is always a bad-weather sport, but because heavy weather adds an extra dimension to the birds' environment. Not many animals anywhere in the world can function in extreme weather as well as ducks and geese.

Here, I was mainly interested in wind. As you can see, it's a fairly bright day, but the wind is powerful, probably cold as well, and even birds as strong as Canada geese have to work their way against it.

(Detail) In most of my paintings of waterfowl, I depict the birds in flight, which is the way you usually see them in the wild. And whenever you see a flying bird, you don't see every individual feather. Still, the characteristics of plumage, wings, feet, head, etc. that I do show, must accurately reflect the species, in this case, Canada geese.

Individuality is another concern. If you look closely at these two geese, you'll see subtle differences in the birds, like the shape of their cheek patches or the amount and intensity of white on their bellies. Like people, every animal is different and capturing that individual character heightens interest and authenticity in a painting.

Fighting the Wind —
Canada Geese,
Oil, 24 x 36, 1985

Years ago, Arnold Krueger and I both tried to establish quail populations on our places in southern Minnesota. Neither of us had a great deal of success at it, but I certainly enjoyed having the birds around and often used my pen quail as subjects for paintings.

In this painting, I tried to capture their various postures, especially the attitudes of their heads, which are quite expressive. It's also interesting to work with the way they fluff and compress their feathers. Quail weigh only six ounces or so, but with their feathers fluffed out against the cold, they can look the size of soccer balls. Other times, especially when they're alarmed, they compress their plumage so tightly that they look bug-eyed. Busy little birds, always pecking at something, fanning their tails, ruffling and preening.

I set this piece in almost exactly the same spot that I used for *Early Winter Morning* (pages 120-121)—a low, rather mucky place that catches runoff from a nearby farm. It's not a very attractive place to people, but the birds liked it.

Hidden Covey — Bobwhite Quail,
Oil, 24 x 32, 1984 (© Brown & Bigelow, 1986)

The gray partridge is another immigrant that has found a good home in the New World. Sometimes called Hungarian partridge, the bird is more widespread in Europe than the name suggests; to English sportsmen, in fact, it holds much the same status as do bobwhites in the American South, usually referred to simply as "bird."

In America, the gray partridge is most plentiful on the grasslands of the Upper Midwest and northern Great Plains, thriving equally well on farmland or the miniature wilderness of sage hills.

Gregarious as quail and at times as hard to approach as a sly cock pheasant, the autumn-colored gray partridge is all an upland hunter could want–strikingly handsome, sporty on the wing, and a delight at the table. Here, David Maass demonstrates its worthiness as subject matter for an artist as well.

Farmland Covey — Gray Partridge,
Oil, 24 x 32, 1983 (© Brown & Bigelow, 1985)

This is Arkansas, which is a sort of funnel for North American ducks. A lot of birds pass through there during the fall, and the hunting is wonderful. I spent a couple of seasons hunting with a fellow from Louisville, who leased about 400 acres between Stuttgart and Pine Bluff. This painting is set there, in a dead reservoir.

Arkansas has three basic types of habitat where the hunting is exceptionally good. One is the ricefield. Another is green timber, which are water-storage areas for the ricefields; green timber is flooded in the fall and winter, the water is drained off in spring to irrigate the rice. In some places, though, the timber is flooded year-round, so the trees die, and the spot becomes a dead reservoir. Ducks like those as resting areas.

Timber Hole — Mallards,
Oil, 26 x 40, 1988

Old apple orchards fascinate me. The trees form all sorts of interesting shapes, and wear and tear as they get older seems to enhance that.

Grouse are so fond of feeding on fruit that they seem the natural subjects for an abandoned-orchard setting. I don't often paint grouse flying toward the viewer, as I did here, but anyone who's hunted grouse knows that having a bird fly straight at you isn't unusual at all.

Orchard Haven — Ruffed Grouse,
Oil, 24 x 32, 1988 (© Brown & Bigelow, 1990)

I did this for the National Wildlife Art Collectors Society, an international organization that sponsors a wildlife art show in Minneapolis each spring. The society chooses an artist of the year, commissions a painting, and sells prints as a fund-raising effort. I was honored in 1982.

This piece is one of my personal favorites. I like to work with backlighting and to paint birds that are partially silhouetted; this allows me to work up a good interplay of both direct and reflected light.

Thundering Out—Ruffed Grouse,
Oil, 24 x 36, 1982

I did this for J.P. Cullen of Janesville, Wisconsin, who commissioned it in memory of Lee Duesterbeck. The setting is Lake Koshkonong in Wisconsin, where Mr. Cullen and the Duesterbeck family have hunted for many years. Specifically, it shows one of their favorite hunting spots, which used to be called Mud Point and has now been renamed Lee's Mud Point, after Lee Duesterbeck.

Ducks Unlimited Canada reproduced this painting in a magnificent book that contains prints by several artists. The large-format books originally sold for $1,500 each, raising a considerable amount of money for DU's wetland projects.

Lee's Point — Canvasbacks,
Oil, 27 x 41, 1986

158

159

This is the last of six paintings in the *Misty Morning* series, which began in 1968 with *Misty Morning—Woodcock*. I didn't know then that it was going to be a series, but when Wild Wings sold out the woodcock print in a surprisingly short time, I did another painting of the same size and basic format. I used ruffed grouse in that one, and it sold even faster.

At that point, Bill Webster and I decided to expand the idea into a series. Over the next three years, I painted four more—mallards, wood ducks, bobwhite quail, and green-winged teal. Those prints were sellouts before the paintings were even finished.

All of the *Misty Morning* pieces have a strong vertical orientation and some sort of open corridor in the center, perhaps a logging trail or an old woods road or just a natural opening. Though never very specific, it helps to lead the viewer into the depth of the painting. In this case, it's a little creek that runs out of the east side of Rice Lake. Lots of willows grow there, and willows grow in shapes that appeal to me as an artist. Teal like to dart around places like this, which is why I chose to show them passing by rather than taking off or landing.

Misty Morning — Green-winged Teal,
Oil, 28 x 24, 1976

My intention here was to show some typical teal habitat with the birds moving through. I also wanted to emphasize the birds' speed, since teal have a reputation as fast fliers — although it may not be entirely justified, since small ducks appear to move faster than they really do.

At any rate, teal seem prone to dropping in someplace for a while, then taking off, circling a few times, and coming down somewhere else. I tried to capture that characteristic by contrasting the foreground birds — moving along full-tilt, as teal do — with the ones in the background getting ready to pitch in.

Morning Mist — Blue-winged Teal,
Oil, 24 x 36, 1984 (Brown & Bigelow, 1986)

riters have more tools in their kits *than artists do. We can choose words that evoke responses among all senses; we can describe sights and smells and tastes and even, through the use of such poetic devices as alliteration, dissonance, and onomatopoeia, reinforce meaning with sheer sound. An artist must appeal directly to the eye, and every response derives from that single sense. A good artist can make us feel the cold inherent to a particular scene, but he has to make us see it first.*

Rippled Landing is a good example of how skillfully David Maass can invoke all the sensory impressions of time, weather and place. This is daybreak in early fall, suffused with cool, low-angle light and the chill of a rising west wind. Duck weather.

Rippled Landing — Redheads,
Oil, 24 x 32, 1986 (© Brown & Bigelow, 1988)

162

The setting here is Pennsylvania, in what seems to be classic turkey habitat. In this painting, I tried to suggest something about how turkeys react to their environment. I imagined that this little flock has been moving through the woods and has come to the stream. I tried to capture the few moments while they decide what to do next, whether they'll take the trouble to fly across or stay on their side and move up or downstream.

Turkeys seem to plan their moves pretty carefully—or at least they give that impression, which is one reason why they're such wonderful game birds.

I also wanted to show a mixed flock, gobblers and hens and a jake, probably a year old and barely bearded.

This painting became the first print of the National Wild Turkey Federation. Besides giving me a chance to do something in support of wild turkey research and conservation, it also meant an opportunity to visit the White House and the Oval Office.

The Wild Turkey Federation gave the No. 1 print to President Carter, and Federation executive Tom Rogers and Bill Webster and I were invited to the White House to make the presentation. We spent about twenty minutes talking with Mr. Carter, who told us about hunting turkeys in Georgia. It was a great honor to be there and to meet him.

Monarchs of the Hardwoods —
Eastern Wild Turkeys,
Oil, 26 x 40, 1980

I did this painting after hunting wild turkey in the Black Hills of South Dakota. Out West, you find the Merriam's subspecies instead of the typical Eastern wild turkey. The differences are subtle but interesting to paint—the Merriam's birds, for instance, have white bars on their tail coverts and tailfeathers as opposed to the buffy, bronzy bars found on eastern turkeys.

The Black Hills is a fascinating place: rocky and rugged and loaded with old pines that have colorful bark and odd-shaped branches that cast intriguing shadows. Working there was a treat, even though I never managed to be in the right place at the right time to shoot a bird. But that's turkey hunting, wherever you are.

Answering the Call — Merriam's Turkey,
Oil, 24 x 32, 1985   (© Brown & Bigelow, 1987)

Woodcock have always intrigued me. I never get tired of painting them, whether they're sitting on the ground in a clutter of leaves or flying in that unique posture. Odd, mysterious little birds. My wife teases me about woodcock paintings, accusing me of just making these birds up; nothing that looks like that could possibly fly.

Like a lot of hunters, I always think of woodcock in terms of experiences I've had with them, and I've had quite a number since that first trip to Pine County about twenty years ago with Bill Webster, wildlife artist Dave Hagerbaumer, and John Dill, a Minneapolis resident and longtime friend.

This is the second of two *Abandoned Orchard* paintings. I got the idea years ago while at Josten's. A salesman and I were traveling through Vermont and New Hampshire, working on a class-ring project for Norwich University, and I'm sure I had the poor man stop the car every five miles or so. I kept seeing places I wanted to photograph for ruffed grouse paintings.

The old apple orchards really intrigued me. The trees were overgrown and obviously not being harvested any longer. Most were about three-quarters dead, but the parts still alive were bearing apples — havens for grouse. I used an old orchard as the setting for a grouse painting about 1980 and decided a few years later to do another, featuring woodcock. The woodcock naturally wouldn't be eating apples, as grouse do, but they'd be there, down on the ground under the trees, feeding on earthworms in the leaf litter and humus.

The trees are great subjects in their own right, twisty old things with a few half-shriveled, wormy apples on them.

Abandoned Orchard — Woodcock,
Oil, 24 x 36, 1984

Many people probably aren't aware of it, but until just recently, entries for the federal duck stamp competition had to be five by seven inches, and prints of the winning design were not always made from the original entry. Enlarging a five-by-seven up to print size, which is six and one-half by nine, can make them look too loose, so the print was often done from a thirteen-by-eighteen repaint of the original. The federal competition now specifies that entries be seven by ten, so now they are seldom repainted.

What you see here is the print from the '82 federal. The repainted version is as close a copy of the original entry as I could do, but of course, the original itself was the result of a fairly long design process, part of which you can see in the drawings at left.

I do a lot of preliminary drawings on tracing paper, not just for stamps but for other paintings as well. I draw each bird individually, perhaps several versions of each one, in different sizes and postures. Then I start laying one over another and moving them around until I find the composition I like best.

The task is to get the birds right, both individually and together. Overlapping birds is extremely important, it seems to me, because it helps unify the design. However, you can get into all sorts of problems, like having a wing that looks like it belongs to the wrong bird; that sort of thing.

As you can see, I tried several different attitudes for the main birds before I settled on what I thought was the strongest design.

I chose canvasbacks as my entry for the '82 federal stamp competition for several reasons: They hadn't been used for a while, were an eligible species that year, and besides, canvasbacks are among my favorite subjects.

The two main birds came from an earlier painting, called *Sweeping the Narrows*. I liked their pose and decided they probably were a strong enough design for a stamp. The judges apparently agreed. That was one of the most gratifying moments of my career.

1982-1983 Migratory Bird Hunting and Conservation Stamp,
Oil, 13 x 18, 1981

1982-83 Federal Preliminary Drawings

*I*f swallows are the harbingers of spring, then to me, goldeneyes bring on winter.

Goldeneyes invariably showed up on Fish Lake from mid to late November, just before freezeup. Mornings and evenings would find them winging around the lake in tight formation, as if they were strengthening their wings for the long journey ahead.

In this painting, the ice has already started to form along shore and it won't be long before we'll wake up one cold, quiet morning to find the entire lake frozen — and the goldeneyes gone.

A Close Pass — Common Goldeneyes,
Oil, 24 x 32, 1982 (© Brown & Bigelow, 1984)

A number of my paintings have strong sentimental value, and this is one of them. It's set in the Weaver Bottoms along the Mississippi River in southwestern Minnesota, where Kelly took me on my first duck hunts.

The Weaver Bottoms appears in many of my earlier paintings, mainly because it was the place I knew best in those days. I haven't painted it much in recent years, but I get the same feeling each time I do, remembering all the hours I spent there with Kelly.

Temporary Stop — Mallards,
Oil, 26 x 38, 1983 (© Brown & Bigelow, 1985)

171

I did a four-painting series showing birds on a winter morning after a fresh snowfall; bobwhites, ruffed grouse, and turkeys appear in the other three.

I had this painting in mind all winter, but I had to wait until April to photograph and study some fresh snow; either I wasn't able to get out right after other snowstorms or we didn't have much snow that year.

The property had been a farm before I bought it, and there was an old, broken-down fence that ran along the edge of a field, which I had planted every year with about two acres of corn for pheasants and deer. I liked the looks of that fence corner, with the old post broken off and rotting away, and I thought it would be an ideal place to put these pheasants.

I was out early that morning, before the snowplow came down the road, and you can see my tracks in the background. It occurred to me that putting the tracks into the painting would explain why the birds are alert. Someone has just walked down the road, and the birds know it. They aren't frightened, but they're keeping an eye out, the rooster especially.

There was quite a bit of wind along with the snow. The sun is fairly intense at that time of year, and the snow tends to crust, so the birds aren't sinking in as much as they would if the snow were softer.

Early Winter Morning — Pheasants,
Oil, 36 x 30, 1983

I wanted this to be late in the day, not sunset but late enough that both the sky and the snow would have a warm, pinkish cast. I also wanted to catch the cold, bleak feeling of a late afternoon in winter. To keep those two, almost contradictory ideas in balance, I arranged the warmer areas — warmer, that is, in color, not necessarily in temperature — between a much cooler sky at the top and an equally cool shadow at the bottom.

I didn't have any great message in mind with this piece, other than perhaps to paint a certain feeling I have about pheasants. Their toughness, particularly their ability to survive harsh winters, always has impressed me. Seeing these two sailing across a snowy, lifeless-looking marsh late in the day suggests a certain optimism; they'll still be there in the morning. And probably next spring, too.

Gliding Away — Pheasants,
Oil, 24 x 32, 1983 (© Brown & Bigelow, 1985)

Year	Title	Initial Price	Edition Size	Publisher
1964	Over the Point – Canvasback (Etching)	—	100	David Maass
1965	Pintail	$16	*60	Shedd Brown
1966	Mallard	16	*60	Shedd Brown
	Grouse	38	*500	Crossroads of Sport
	Canvasbacks	38	*400	Crossroads of Sport
1967	Misty Meadow – Green Wings	16	*60	Shedd Brown
1968	Midwinter Grouse	16	*60	Shedd Brown
1969	Whitewater Cans	16	*60	Shedd Brown
	Coming In – Canada Geese	50	400	Frost & Reed and Crossroads of Sport
1970	After Feeding – Canada Geese	16	*60	Shedd Brown
1971	Back From Feeding – Mallards	60	600	Frost & Reed
	Bogland Covey – Quail	60	600	Frost & Reed
1972	Misty Morning – Woodcock	50	450	Wild Wings
1973	Among the Pines – Quail	40	600	Wild Wings
	Back Bay – Mallards	40	600	Wild Wings
	Breaking In – Bluebills	55	480	Wild Wings
	Breaking Weather – Canada Geese	55	580	Wild Wings
	Misty Morning – Ruffed Grouse	55	580	Wild Wings
1974	Autumn Birch – Woodcock	70	580	Wild Wings
	Misty Morning – Wood Ducks	55	580	Wild Wings
	On the Move – Canvasbacks	60	580	Wild Wings
	Ridge Line – Ruffed Grouse	70	580	Wild Wings
	River Flats – Pintails	60	580	Wild Wings
	1974-75 Federal Duck Stamp – Wood Ducks	100	*2,800	David Maass
	The King of Ducks – Canvasbacks	—	600	Ducks Unlimited
1975	Dusk in the Bay – Canada Geese	50	600	Wild Wings
	Misty Morning – Mallards	85	580	Wild Wings
	Misty Morning – Quail	85	580	Wild Wings
	Redhead Bay	70	580	Wild Wings
	Twisting Through – Blue-winged Teal	70	580	Wild Wings
1976	Hasty Departure – Ruffed Grouse	70	580	Wild Wings
	Misty Morning – Green-winged Teal	85	580	Wild Wings
	Over the Pond – Ruffed Grouse	53	600	Wild Wings
	Placid Backwaters – Wood Ducks	70	580	Wild Wings
	Sweeping the Narrows – Canvasbacks	70	580	Wild Wings
	Western Marsh – Pintails	70	580	Wild Wings
	Winter Winds – Bluebills	70	580	Wild Wings
1977	Autumn Day – Ruffed Grouse	100	850	Wild Wings
	Autumn Marsh – Mallards	75	580	Wild Wings
	Back Country Ruffs	75	580	Wild Wings
	Covey Break – Quail	75	580	Wild Wings
	Early Arrivals – Mallards	55	850	Wild Wings
	Into the Shallows – Canada Geese	75	580	Wild Wings
	River's Edge – Mallards	75	580	Wild Wings
	1977 Minnesota Duck Stamp – Mallards	100	*2,800	David Maass
1978	Cautious Trio – Turkey	75	850	Wild Wings
	Deadwood Corner – Mallards	85	850	Wild Wings
	December Squall – Pheasants	75	850	Wild Wings
	First Pass – Mallards	85	850	Wild Wings
	Marshland – Canada Geese	75	850	Wild Wings
	New Snow – Ruffed Grouse	85	850	Wild Wings
	Swinging the Channel – Canvasbacks	85	850	Wild Wings
	Woodland Repose – Ruffed Grouse	100	850	Wild Wings
	Working the Bay – Bluebills	85	850	Wild Wings
1979	Autumn Day – Woodcock	100	850	Wild Wings
	Grouse Cover	100	850	Wild Wings
	Heavy Weather – Redheads	100	850	Wild Wings
1979	Monarch of the Hardwoods	$125	950	National Wild Turkey Federation
	Monarch of the Hardwoods (President's Edition)	1,000	100	National Wild Turkey Federation
	Pintails in Autumn	50	950	Wild Wings
	Reelfoot Visitors at Middlefork Club	100	850	Wild Wings
	1979 Minnesota Duck Stamp – Pintails	110	3,800	David Maass
1980	Abandoned Orchard – Ruffed Grouse	125	850	Wild Wings
	After the Rain – Bobwhite	100	850	Wild Wings
	Canvasbacks in Autumn	50	950	Wild Wings
	Into Quiet Waters – Mallards	100	850	Wild Wings
	Mallards in Autumn	50	950	Wild Wings
	North Shore – Goldeneyes	100	850	Wild Wings
	Ruffed Grouse in Autumn	50	950	Wild Wings
	Two-Away Woodcock	85	850	Wild Wings
	1980 Ruffed Grouse Society Stamp	100	1,380	Ruffed Grouse Society
	Turkey Vulture – Cathartes aura	100	777	Buzzard Council
1981	Backwater Hideaway – Wood Ducks	150	950	Wild Wings
	Early Winter Morning – Bobwhite	150	850	Wild Wings
	Farm Pond – Green-winged Teal	125	850	Wild Wings
	Jimmy's Point – Delta Marsh Bluebills	125	950	Wild Wings
	Low Ceiling – Canada Geese	100	850	Wild Wings
	Sunlit Marsh – Mallards	125	950	Wild Wings
	Timber's Edge – Ruffed Grouse	150	950	Wild Wings
	Wild Wings Logo – Green-winged Teal	75	950	Wild Wings
	Quiet Corner – Wood Ducks	—	400	North Carolina Chapter – DU
	On the River – Wood Ducks	—	400	North Carolina Chapter – DU
	1981 Wild Turkey Stamp	125	3,200	National Wild Turkey Federation
	Wildlife Heritage – Ruffed Grouse	85	500	Minnesota Wildlife Heritage Foundation
1982	Early Winter Morning – Ruffed Grouse	150	950	Wild Wings
	Saskatchewan Greenheads	125	950	Wild Wings
	Thundering Out – Ruffed Grouse	125	900	Wildlife and Western Art Show
	Windswept Marsh – Canvasbacks	150	950	Wild Wings
	1982-83 Federal Duck Stamp – Canvasbacks	135	22,250	David Maass
	1982 Bobwhite Quail Stamp	125	3,900	International Quail Foundation
1983	1983 Minnesota Turkey Stamp – Whitewater Valley Gobblers	125	1,500	Minnesota Chapter – Wild Turkey Federation and Wild Wings
	1983 Arkansas Duck Stamp – Green-winged Teal	125	7,200	Grisham's
	Early Winter Morning – Pheasant	150	950	Wild Wings
	Greenhead Country	200	3,600	Minnesota Chapter – Ducks Unlimited
	Hillside Flush – Ruffed Grouse	125	950	Wild Wings
	Into the Cove – Canada Geese	125	950	Wild Wings
1984	Canvasbacks on the Delta Marsh	45	1,000	North American Wildlife Foundation
	Canvasbacks on the Delta Marsh	125	750	North American Wildlife Foundation
	Canvasbacks on the Delta Marsh	275	200	North American Wildlife Foundation
	Edge of the Marsh – Pintails	125	950	Wild Wings

* Approximately

Year	Title	Initial Price	Edition Size	Publisher
1984	On the Move – Mallards	$50	1,500	Wild Wings
	Sheltered Hideaway – Wood Ducks	125	950	Wild Wings
	Woodlot Flush – Ruffed Grouse	50	1,500	Wild Wings
	1984 Maine Duck Stamp – Black Ducks	135	11,115	Wild Wings and State of Maine
	1984 Texas Duck Stamp – Wood Ducks	125	9,400	Collector's Covey and State of Texas
	1984 Missouri Wild Turkey Stamp	125	1,500	Grisham's
	1984 North Dakota Duck Stamp – Canvasbacks	135	3,438	Sporten Art and State of North Dakota
1985	Abandoned Orchard – Woodcock	125	850	Wild Wings
	Early Winter Morning – Turkey	150	950	Wild Wings
	Low Ceiling – Snows and Blues	100	850	Wild Wings
	Swinging In – Mallards	125	650	Wild Wings
	Willow Point – Redheads	85	950	Wild Wings
	1985 Hunting Heritage Stamp – Canada Geese	125	2,400	Wildlife Legislative Fund of America and Collector's Covey
	1985 New Jersey Duck Stamp – Mallards	135	10,011	Sporten Art
	1985 Maine Duck Stamp – Common Eiders	135	2,330	Wild Wings and State of Maine
1986	Autumn Mist – Ruffed Grouse	125	850	Wild Wings
	Canadas in the Rye	85	650	Wild Wings
	Fighting the Wind – Canada Geese	125	850	Wild Wings
	Homestead Covey – Bobwhite	125	650	Wild Wings
	Mallards – Central Flyway	125	700	Wild Wings
	A Touch of Winter – Pheasants	125	850	Wild Wings
	Early Spring Covey – Bobwhite	125	3,900	International Quail Foundation
	1986 New York Duck Stamp – Mallards	135	14,040	National Wildlife Galleries and Petersen Prints
	1986 Maine Duck Stamp – Wood Ducks	135	1,815	Wild Wings and State of Maine
	1986 Texas Wild Turkey Stamp	125	1,500	Collector's Covey
	1986 Ducks Unlimited Stamp – Green-winged Teal	—	5,000	Ducks Unlimited
1987	Late Migration – Bluebills	125	480	Wild Wings
	A New Day – Cardinals	95	850	Wild Wings
	Pintails – Pacific Flyway	125	700	Wild Wings
	1987 Ruffed Grouse Society Stamp – Woodcock	125	1,380	Ruffed Grouse Society
	Eastern Shore Goldeneyes	135	1,200	Chesapeake Bay Conservation and Russell A. Fink
	1987 Arkansas Turkey Stamp	130	1,500	Grisham's and Arkansas Chapter – National Wild Turkey Federation
	Delta Dinner Canvasback	—	300	Wild Wings and North American Wildlife Foundation
	Lee's Point – Canvasbacks	—	1,250	Canada Ducks Unlimited
	Windy Point – Bluebills	200	4,000	Wisconsin Chapter – Ducks Unlimited
1988	Low Ceiling – White Fronted Geese	100	850	Wild Wings
	Cold Front – Canvasbacks	125	850	Wild Wings

Year	Title	Initial Price	Edition Size	Publisher
1988	November Winds – Canvasbacks	$90	950	California Waterfowl Association
	Morning Shadows – Ruffed Grouse	125	850	Wild Wings
	Timber Hole – Mallards	145	1,200	Wild Wings
	Canyon Crossing – Ruffed Grouse	145	1,200	Wild Wings
	Wood Ducks – Mississippi Flyway	125	700	Wild Wings
	Late Break – Canadas	200	1,800	Iowa Chapter – Ducks Unlimited
	Greenhead Alert – Mallards	—	5,300	Ducks Unlimited
	Canada Salute – Canada Geese	—	1,750	Ducks Unlimited
1989	Solitary Woodcock	145	950	Wild Wings
	Stone Barn – Pheasants	145	1,500	Wild Wings
	Autumn Shades – Wood Ducks	145	1,200	Wild Wings
	Green Timber – Mallards	145	1,500	Wild Wings
	1989 North American Waterfowl Management Plan Stamp – Wood Ducks	145	—	Ducks Unlimited and Petersen Prints
	1989 Texas Duck Stamp Print – Mallards	135	5,650	Collector's Covey and State of Texas